ENDORSEMENTS

"This book is one of a kind. There are many books that are compilations of articles, instruments, and exercises, but Hultman's has a theme—values—which makes it unique. Moreover, the book represents a lifetime of important work on values. Thus, for OD consultants and our clients, we now have in one volume an invaluable tool kit for values work. And when have we ever needed such a tool any more than now? Values work is more important than ever before. Here is our source for this work."

—**W. Warner Burke**, Edward Lee Thorndike Professor of Psychology and Education, Teachers College, Columbia University

"Ken Hultman is a first rate scholar and advocate of the importance of humanitarian values at the level of the individual, the small group, or an entire organization. His ability to distill and synthesize a great deal of social science theory and translate it into a language and frameworks that we can all understand is masterful. Organizational development consultants who are looking for practical tools and techniques to use in doing their work with individuals, teams or whole organizations will find this book to be full of ready-to-use instruments all of which are simply explained and grounded in solid social science theory."

—**Tony Petrella**, Organizational Consultant and Executive Coach

"This pragmatic collection of tools and articles puts *values* into the very conversations and change activities that they truly belong in. They help make overt the deep impact *values* have in our work, and how essential it is to make them conscious."

—**Linda Ackerman Anderson**, Co-Founder, Being First, Inc.

"Both a practical workbook and a comprehensive text, Hultman's new book will appeal to newcomers and seasoned veterans alike. It is of utmost importance that we bring values back to center stage in our change work, and this volume is a major step toward bringing this about."

—**John D. Adams, Ph.D.**, Chair and Professor, Organizational Systems Ph.D. Program, Saybrook Graduate School

DISCLAIMER:

VALUES-DRIVEN CHANGE

VALUES-DRIVEN CHANGE

Strategies and Tools for Long-Term Success

Ken Hultman

Foreword by Bill Gellermann

iUniverse, Inc.
New York Lincoln Shanghai

Values-Driven Change
Strategies and Tools for Long-Term Success

Copyright © 2006 by Kenneth E. Hultman

iUniverse books may be ordered through booksellers or by contacting:

iUniverse
2021 Pine Lake Road, Suite 100
Lincoln, NE 68512
www.iuniverse.com
1-800-Authors (1-800-288-4677)

ISBN-13: 978-0-595-39394-7 (pbk)
ISBN-13: 978-0-595-83792-2 (ebk)
ISBN-10: 0-595-39394-2 (pbk)
ISBN-10: 0-595-83792-1 (ebk)

Printed in the United States of America

Permissions

To Bill Gellermann
Who set the values bar for OD

CONTENTS

FOREWORD

Values, Context, Vision, and Strategy

It has been said, "The key to strategy is context," and that idea provides the framework for thinking about the fundamental importance of "values" in establishing context. This book explores the concept of "values" and provides many ways to help individuals, groups, and organizations clarify their values. In this *Foreword*, we begin by reviewing the context within which values, purpose or mission, vision, and strategy (goals, objectives, and plans) exist, with values being the most fundamental, because they shape mission, vision, vision, strategy, and all the elements of strategy. And, in what may seem paradoxical, values provide the context for values.

About Context

Context can be conceived as the meanings or circumstances surrounding a concept that gives it meaning. So, as just noted, values, purpose and vision provide context for strategy (goals, objectives, and plans). In other words, values, purpose, and vision provide the meaningful background for formulating strategic goals, objectives, and action plans.

About Values

Values can be conceived as "standards of importance" and those standards shape the most fundamental concepts on which context is based, namely *purpose or mission, vision,* and *values.* It is also helpful to recognize that these three concepts are interrelated: namely values shape purpose, which shapes vision, which shapes values, and so on. And those interrelations are dynamic in that as one changes, it can influence the others to change. For example, if one's purpose in life shifts from seeking a good life for one's self to seeking a good life for all, that person's values and vision will also change. Examples of values include: life, liberty, and the "pursuit of happiness," with "happiness" conceived as it was by Aristotle, namely as "a whole life well-lived." In this connection, for a particular individual, we also need to know whether the "life" being focused on is his/her own life or the life of a larger group (e.g. family, organization, or community).

About Purpose/Mission

From the point of view of an individual, purpose or mission refers to his/her answer to the question, "What is your reason for being?" And the same question applies to groups, organizations and other collections of people who share a collective identity (e.g. team member, organization member, "New Yorker," "American," or "global citizen"). Values are fundamental to defining and conceiving purpose. For example, in thinking about the purpose of a business organization and its members, do they conceive their purpose as being "to maximize value for shareholders" or "to serve the interests of stakeholders (including shareholders, customers, workers, and communities)?" People's answers to the question about purpose give meaning to their lives. Example: Wisconsin Public Service Corporation conceives of its mission as: "Provide customers with the best value in energy and related services."

About Vision

Purpose can be translated into a vision, namely the answer to the question, "What will life be like if you are successful in serving your purpose?" and that answer will be expressed as words that evoke an image or a collection of images. For example, Wisconsin Public Service Corporation (whose mission was just given) describes its vision as: "People creating the world's premier energy company." It then expanded on the images intended by those words:

- *People.* All employees sharing a commitment to work together, and with customers and suppliers, to become the World's Premier Energy Company.

- *Creating.* Employees immersing themselves in the excitement of continuously inventing and improving products and services in a world of ever-changing needs, expectations, and demands.

- *World's Premier Energy Company.* An organization that, in the eyes of customers and all others, creates best-value services and products for customers, constantly improves, and respects all people. Its employees share common beliefs, are committed to a common purpose and quality, and are highly skilled."

Another example of vision is by Levi Strauss & Co., "...responsible commercial success in the eyes of our constituencies, which include stockholders, employees, consumers, customers, suppliers, and communities..."

About Culture

Culture has been conceived as "the way we do things around here" and that "way" is shaped by **beliefs** (assumptions about reality), **values** (standards of importance as described above), and **norms** (standards of behavior based on values). Examples: **beliefs**—people must be motivated to do their jobs by promises of reward or threats of punishment and the purpose of business is to maximize profit; **values**—profit for stockholders is more important than a "living wage" for workers; **norms**—do not lie, cheat or steal. What are some of the beliefs, values, and norms that would be reflected in your vision of an ideal organization?

About Strategy

Strategy refers to the goals, objectives, and action plans that will move people (individuals, groups, organizations, etc.) from shared purpose and vision to action aimed at serving the purpose and bringing the vision into being.

- **About goals.** In thinking about how to realize vision (bring it into being), it can help by first thinking about the kinds of things that need to be accomplished in general terms, in order to achieve our goals and objectives. An example might be, "To develop a strategic planning process enabling us to achieve a high level of motivation by all of our organization members."

- **About objectives.** In thinking about achieving general goals, it can help to define the specific objectives that will enable achievement of the goals. That involves specifying the results to be accomplished, including specific target dates (or time periods). For example, "Conduct strategic planning meetings for each department involving all department members in setting general goals, specifying objectives (and target dates), and specifying individual responsibilities for accomplishing each objective."

- **About action plans.** In thinking about accomplishing each objective, it can help to map our specific action steps (with target dates or time periods along with responsible individuals or groups) that combine to make accomplishment possible by the time specified in the objective.

- **About a strategic plan** In combination, a set of general goals, specific objectives, and action plans for accomplishing each of the objectives are called a "strategic plan."

The interrelationship among all of these elements, which provide context for thinking about values, can be described in this way:

Figure 1
Context for Thinking about Values

PURPOSE (mission)
(reason for being)

VISION
(image of desired reality)

CURRENT REALITY

CULTURE (shared beliefs, values, and norms that affect "the way we do things around here")
- **Beliefs** (assumptions, models, ways of thinking about reality)
- **Values** (standards of importance)
- **Norms** (standards of behavior based on values)

STRATEGY
- **Strategic goals** (general direction)
- **Strategic objectives** (specific results/times)
- **Action Plans** (what, when and who to achieve objectives)

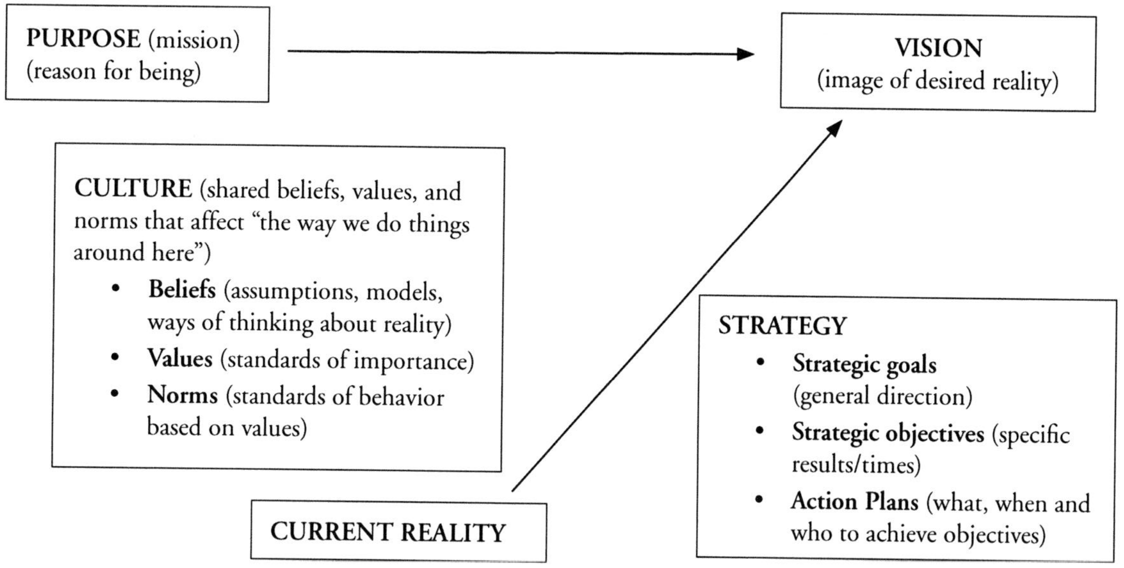

As a whole, this model describes ways of thinking about valuing and acting to help individuals, groups, and organizations focus on their reason for being (purpose/mission), the way they would like things to be (their vision or desired reality), their current reality, and their strategy (general goals, specific objectives, and action plans) for moving in the direction of their vision. Much as a compass gives direction to people traveling in unfamiliar territory, the relationship between current reality and vision of desired reality can give general direction and strategy (goals, objectives and plans) give more precise guidance for moving in the desired direction. As noted, values are the most fundamental element in choosing how each of us will set our inner compass. And, from the point of view of an organization (or any other human system), *shared* values are the most important element in setting people's inner compass so they can travel *together*. This book is not only about understanding values, but also about *using that understanding*. To serve that purpose, it provides numerous inventories, exercises, and articles that will help readers translate their understanding into *doing*.

Bill Gellermann, Ph.D.

Co-author, with Mark Frankel and Robert Ladenson,

Values and Ethics in Organization and Human Systems Development

(Jossey-Bass, 1990)

PREFACE

I've had a passion for the study of values my entire professional career. The question of what *really* matters in life has been and is an enduring and often haunting theme. While I was a graduate student at Rutgers University I did my doctoral dissertation on the impact of a leader's values on members' behavior in small groups. Following that I began focusing on the role of values in resistance to personal and organizational change. Gradually this evolved into a larger study of values as drivers of corporate culture and change. A lot has been written in recent years about building "values-based" cultures. The fact is that all organizational cultures are based on values, but not all values are created equal. Recent research has consistently found that certain values are associated with higher levels of performance, whether performance is measured in terms of financial criteria such as stock returns or revenue growth, or by corporate longevity and sustainability.

Another misnomer is that values are synonymous with ethics or morality. Often when leaders assert that their organizations are "values-based," what they mean is that they operate by high ethical standards. The fact is, however, that values are standards for all types of behavior, not only ethical behavior. Once values are identified they then must be defined behaviorally and embedded in action. For individuals, this means that espoused values will guide action. For teams and organizations, it means embedding values in key management systems, such as strategy, employee selection, day-to-day supervision, and the performance evaluation process. This represents a process of continuous improvement and must be managed in the same way as any other aspect of organizational functioning.

In this book I will use the term "values-driven," instead of "values-based," to stress the role of values in the change process. My objective for this project was to compile everything I've written on organizational values and change in a single text, so it would be more widely available. While most of the material has been published previously, everything has been updated and revised. The book is organized into four parts: values-driven team change, values-driven personal change, values-driven organizational change, and values-driven multi-level change (i.e. applications that can be used at the personal, team, and organizational levels). Each chapter presents both theoretical concepts and practical tools, organized more like a workbook than a traditional chapter. Seven proven non-standardized instruments are included, in addition to structured facilitation processes and exercises. All tools come with a complete set of instructions. Included are resources that can be used in coaching, team building, training programs on values and culture, and large-scale organization development or culture change.

The only piece not authored by me is the article in Appendix 1 on values-driven conflict resolution by George J. McCall, Professor Emeritus at the University of Missouri, Saint Louis. In 1964 I took a seminar taught by George on social group theory. Some of the initial seeds for the material in this volume were planted during that seminar, so I invited George to submit his ideas on conflict resolution, which represent an emerging interest of his, and a topic of great importance to change facilitators. George's article has enhanced the substance of this book, and I greatly appreciate his contribution.

As you plan and implement your next change effort, I hope you find these resources helpful in achieving your goals. I believe if we can challenge organizations to take the high ground in their principles and practices, we are helping to create a healthier and more sustainable world. What could be a nobler calling?

I'd like to acknowledge the people who helped me with this project. My wife, Pat, not only suggested this compilation, but also served as its editor. Over our 33 years of marriage, she's not only made me a better writer but also a better thinker and a better person. Bill Gellermann offered many useful suggestions for improvement and also wrote the Foreword. For his generous help to me personally, and for his lifetime contribution to the field of OD, I'm pleased to dedicate this book to him. Kristine Quade provided a detailed review of the manuscript, and helped me narrow down my initial 29 chapters to 8. If the book has become more "user friendly," it is due largely to Kristine's input. I'd also like to thank Debra Dinnocenzo for suggesting the book's title, and Micah Janus for suggestion the contrast between change-driven values and values-driven change. Finally, I'd like to thank my colleagues Linda Ackerman-Anderson, John Adams, Warner Burke, and Tony Petrella for putting their professional reputations on the line by endorsing the book. I hope the book is worthy of their confidence.

Ken Hultman

March, 2006

INTRODUCTION

PURPOSE: To define the terms value and values-driven change.

What Are Values?

A value is a standard of importance based on beliefs (Gellermann, Frankel, & Ladenson, 1990). A value system is a hierarchical ordering of values along a continuum of relative importance. Once embraced, values play an executive role in personality and organizational culture, serving as criteria for making decisions and setting priorities. Values are to people what instincts are to animals. Without the capacity to formulate and act on values, life on the human level would not exist.

It will be useful to discuss briefly the role of values in personality, before describing their role in culture. The purpose of behavior is to meet needs, and values are preferred ways of meeting needs. While people have a variety of needs, it's the values they choose to address their psychological and social needs that have the greatest impact on behavior in the workplace. Milton Rokeach (1973) maintained that the ultimate purpose of our value system, as well as all our other attitudes and beliefs, is to maintain and enhance our self-conceptions, or what we refer to as self-worth. He distinguished between *terminal values* and *instrumental values.* Terminal values define the overall goal we want to achieve and have two components: our purpose or personal mission defines *why* we exist, and our dreams for the future or personal vision defines *what* we want to become. We have a current self-image (who we are now) and an idealized self-image (who we want to become). Terminal values inspire us to move toward the latter.

Instrumental values are preferred modes of conduct, defining *how* we plan to fulfill our purpose and dreams. When people use the term "value" they're usually referring to instrumental values, and this is how the term will be used in the remainder of this article. These values focus on *competence*, which focuses on abilities, and integrity, which focuses on *character.* We're not only industrious problem-solvers but also ethical and moral beings, concerned with questions about good and bad, right and wrong. In order to preserve and enhance our self-worth, therefore, we must perceive ourselves and be perceived by others as both capable and ethical. Competence and character have both a personal and social dimension, allowing us to distinguish four sub-needs:

- **Personal competence**—People need to view themselves and be viewed by others as being skilled, knowledgeable, and capable.

- **Social competence**—People need to view themselves and be viewed by others as making a difference.

- **Personal character**—People need to view themselves and be viewed by others as being ethical and moral; this is a requirement for self-respect.

- **Social character**—People need to be accepted by others.

Values are psychological constructs, within the mind of a person. Organizations as such don't have values, but they have cultures and those cultures are shaped by values that are shared in varying degrees. The shaping can go both ways, individual to organization or organization to individual, though the latter tends to be more powerful. Terminal values reflect corporate mission (purpose) and vision (dream), while instrumental values are standards for serving the mission and vision.

A primary function of an organization's value system is to maintain and enhance its members' collective sense of self-esteem, or what we call *morale*. A strong connection exists between an organization's level of morale, and both its vision and the instrumental values it employs to move toward that vision. Organizations with low morale have trouble getting people fired up about some lofty vision, and tend to use instrumental values that focus on short-term survival and fire fighting. In contrast, organizations with high morale have an easier time building commitment toward vision, and use instrumental values that focus on long-range growth. Factors contributing to low morale must be identified and remedied before an organization can sustain a positive effort toward vision. Once progress is made in this area, the focus can shift to selecting and embedding instrumental values that foster growth.

What Is Values-Driven Change?

As criteria for making decisions and setting priorities, values are meant to be considered before taking action. In response to external pressures, however, organizations often allow change to drive values rather than the other way around. This practice increases their vulnerability to making changes they later regret, when they win a battle only to lose the war. As can be seen in Table 1, the differences between the two approaches are startling and have far reaching implications for individuals, teams, and organizations. Throughout the book, I will advocate values-driven change for individuals, teams, and organizations.

Table 1

Change-Driven Values versus Values-Driven Change

Change-Driven Values	Values-Driven Change
Reactive	Proactive
Emphasis on damage control	Emphasis on forward movement, growth
Problems	Opportunities
Focus on the urgent	Focus on the crucial
Short-term perspective	Long-term perspective
Narrow-minded, insular view	Open-minded, broad view
Anxiety-driven	Mission, vision-driven
Emotional, impulsive	Rational, deliberate
Expedient criteria	Established criteria
Imposed, stakeholders unaligned	Participatory, stakeholders aligned
Uncertainty, confusion	Confidence in direction, outcomes

P A R T 1

VALUES-DRIVEN TEAM CHANGE

1. **Removing Barriers to Team Effectiveness**

   Provides a theoretical framework for understanding barriers to team effectiveness, and the Psychological Need Fulfillment Inventory™, which can be used to assess and resolve team problems.

2. **Building Team Trust**

   Discusses the dynamics of trust and mistrust, provides the Trust Scale and Plan for Building Trust, which can be used to assess and build team trust.

1

REMOVING BARRIERS TO TEAM EFFECTIVENESS

PURPOSE: To provide a theoretical framework and tool for assessing and resolving team problems.

Psychological Needs in the Workplace

All behavior is purposeful, and that purpose is to meet needs. Understanding needs is a prerequisite to understanding values, because values are the cognitive representations of needs (Rokeach, 1973). Essentially, an organization is a group of people working together to meet their needs. The most effective way to gain insight into human behavior is to ask, "What need are these people trying to meet?" Needs are experienced as internal urges and desires. An unfulfilled need is accompanied by pain or discomfort, which can be physical, emotional, psychological or spiritual, depending on the need. Fulfilling a need, in contrast, produces either pleasure or relief from pain. People are not islands unto themselves, capable of meeting their needs in isolation from others; the process of meeting needs requires them to interact with the world and with other people.

Trying to get our needs met is always precarious because we can never be sure that our efforts will produce the desired result. Whenever we want something we face a predicament, because there's always the possibility that we won't be able to get it. Attempting to meet needs requires us to step into the future, where there is risk associated with everything we do—uncertainty is one of the certainties of life. No matter how carefully we plan, we are *vulnerable* to having bad things happen. Acting on needs within a context of vulnerability is constant and we're aware of it to some extent before we act, either consciously or sub-consciously, such awareness produces anxiety and fear. Since our vulnerability is part of our human reality. Since our vulnerability is constant and we're aware of it to some extent before we act, either consciously or sub-consciously, such awareness produces anxiety and fear. Most of us get use to this and regard it as normal, until the level of perceived risk begins to intensify. This is significant because, in addition to desire, fear is also a powerful source of motivation. In the struggle to get our needs met desire and fear walk hand in hand, and one is always capable of overpowering the other.

Faced with this dilemma, in any given situation there are four courses of action open to us. We can either:

- **Escape** something we perceive is dangerous.
- **Avoid** something we perceive is dangerous.
- **Attack** something we perceive is dangerous.
- **Pursue** something we believe is important.

Escaping, avoiding, and attacking are primarily defensive, self-protective courses of action. Perceiving something or someone as dangerous evokes fear, triggering the well-known *fight-flight* response. *Escaping* and *avoiding* are flight responses, while *attacking* is a fight response. In situations where a real danger exists, such responses are often very appropriate, and may even be necessary for survival. There are many times, however, when escaping, avoiding or attacking are counter-productive. People often escape situations they should face, avoid opportunities that could help them learn, and attack people with whom they should be building alliances. While escaping, avoiding, and attacking may allow us to deal with an immediate danger, they do nothing to help us make something positive happen. Also, these responses do nothing to remove our basic vulnerability as human being. After the danger has passed, we still have to face anxiety and take risks if we intend to get our needs met.

Another problem is that our nervous system can't distinguish between real and imagined danger, and reacts the same way under both sets of circumstances—with fear. Accordingly, the perception of danger will make us afraid, even if there's nothing to be afraid of. We are also capable of overreacting to real danger, making mountains out of molehills. I work with people in organizations who are afraid to give presentations in front of others. When I ask them to explain the reason, they often say that they worry about making fools out of themselves. Sometimes the anxiety is so intense that they literally can't say anything; they choke on their words. I challenge them to reevaluate the danger and put it into a more realistic perspective. I also point out that this type of anxiety will keep them from achieving their career potential, and challenge them to overcome it. If they're willing to try, I then take them through some exercises designed to desensitize the anxiety. Perceived danger, both real and imagined, not only inhibits people's performance, but it is also one of the primary reasons for resistance to change.

Of the four courses of action available to us only *pursuing* is proactive and non-defensive; it focuses on making good things happen instead of preventing bad things from happening. Pursuing is related to *empowerment*. To pursue something means facing our vulnerability and taking the risks necessary to achieve our goals. It's only by pursuing that we can successfully meet our needs, while doing what we believe is important in life. As we weigh our options in any given situation, therefore, each of us must answer this question: Am I going to live my life or let fear live it for me?

According to Maslow (1968), needs exist in a hierarchy of relative pre-potency, with physiological needs at the bottom, followed in order by safety, social, psychological, and self-actualization needs. He maintains that once people's lower-level needs are met, they focus on their higher-level needs. Since the nature of lower level physiological and safety needs are rather obvious, I will focus on the powerful, but more subtle influence of social, psychological, and self-actualization needs of people in the workplace.

My formulation is different from Maslow's in that I view social, psychological and self-actualization needs as serving the overall purpose of allowing people to view themselves and be viewed by others as having worth and value as a person—the mega-goal of personality. Social psychologist William McDougal (1926) referred to self-worth as "the master sentiment." Many other psychologists have discussed the centrality of our need to maintain and enhance our self-worth. The perception of being worthwhile instills one with a feeling of hope, while the perception of lacking worth gives one a feeling of despair. When people feel bad about themselves it's hard to get them to do anything. If you're interested in motivating people, the single most effective approach is to help them have a more positive self-image, so they can motivate themselves.

Everything we do reflects on our worth, one way or another. In any given situation we are motivated to validate our worth but since we can never be sure what's going to happen next, we're also vulnerable to having our sense of worth lowered. Therefore, although the need for worth can propel us forward, fear of unworthiness can also cause us to hold back.

Because having a sense of worth is our central need, other social, psychological, and self actualization needs serve as means to this end. We strive for a sense of worth through what psychologists have called the "drive for greatness," which focuses on competence, and the "drive for goodness," which focuses on character or integrity. To feel worthy, therefore, people must believe that they are both competent and ethical. Competence and character have both a personal and social dimension, allowing us to distinguish four sub-needs that serve the overall purpose of helping us validate our worth as human beings: mastery, a sense of meaning and purpose, respect and acceptance. In my experience, these are the needs most responsible for people's behavior in organizations. Although all four needs assert themselves more or less simultaneously, at any point in time one will usually be more powerful than the others. These needs are displayed graphically in Figure 1.1.

Mastery (Personal Competence)

People need to view themselves and be viewed by others as being competent and capable. This is what David McClelland (1975) refers to as the need for achievement. Frederick Herzberg (1966) lists achievement, responsibility, advancement and the work itself as four of his five job satisfiers, all of which are indicators of one's competence. Mastery is personal in focus, because the emphasis is on what we're capable of doing. The perception of being competent produces feelings of self-confidence and pride, increasing one's sense of worth, while the perception of being incompetent produces feelings of self-doubt and shame, lowering one's sense of worth. Although people have a need for mastery, they are also motivated by the fear of failure, which can cause them to avoid or escape situations where they anticipate poor performance. This can keep them from taking the risks necessary to develop and use their talents and abilities.

While everyone in organizations wants to view themselves and be viewed by others as competent, I have been struck by how quickly people judge each other as being either competent or incompetent. Although they rarely disclose their thoughts about this to each other, when they meet with me privately they're very quick to make statements like these:

"They should never have selected him for that job."

"His incompetence is dragging all of us down."

"If they were hiring people based on merit, she never would have gotten that job."

"I don't know why they promoted him. There are many others around here more qualified."

When facilitating team building, I deliberately bring the issue of competence out in the open so it can be discussed directly, because people's confidence in each other's ability is often a key to developing cohesiveness. My goal is to move team members from judging each other's competence to offering the support and encouragement that would make the team more effective. Teams perform better when members strive to help each other increase their competence.

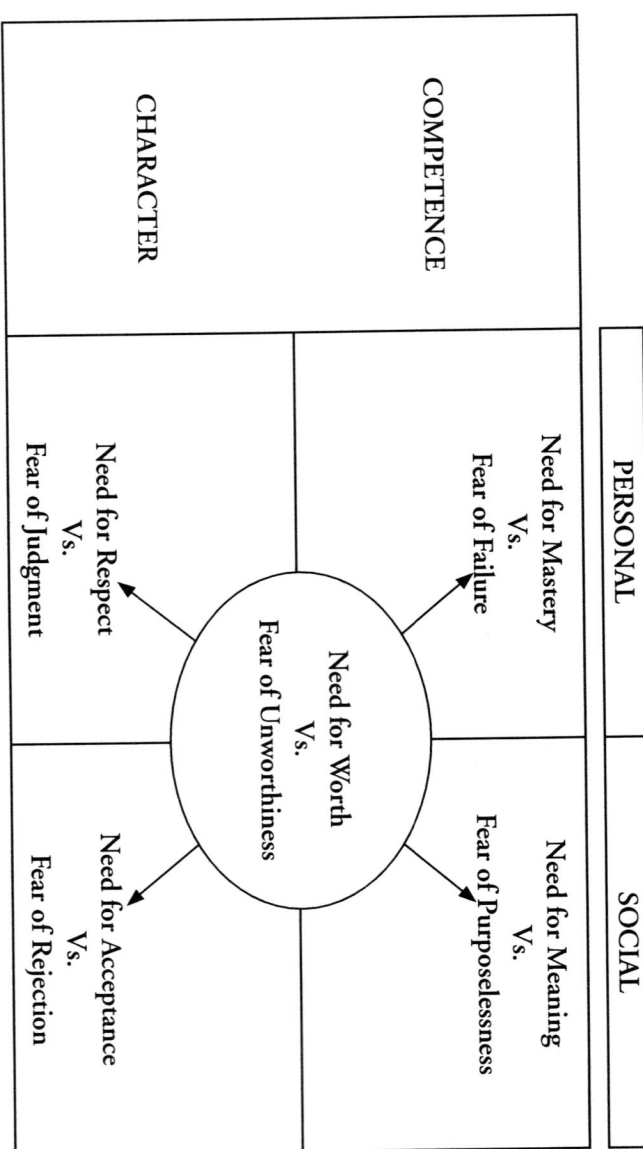

Figure 1.1
Psychological Needs

A Sense of Meaning and Purpose (Social Competence)

People need to view themselves and be viewed by others as making a contribution to the team/organization, and their feeling of contribution is heightened by their sense of organizational worth, a sense that their organization is serving a purpose (mission) that they consider important. People not only need to feel that they've done a good job, but also feel that their work is important. Herzberg mentioned recognition for achievement as his other job satisfier, which is an indication that one's work is purposeful. Other writers refer to this as pride of accomplishment. A sense of meaning and purpose is social in emphasis, because it has to do with people's desire to leave the organization better off than when they arrived. More than any other, this need addresses the question, "Why am I here?" The perception of making a contribution produces feelings of well-being and fulfillment, enhancing one's sense of worth, while the perception of not making a contribution brings feelings of depression, emptiness, and discouragement, lowering one's sense of worth. Although people have a need for a sense of meaning and purpose, they can also be motivated by a fear that their work will be insignificant, leading them either to search compulsively for ways of making a more important contribution, or give in to a sense of uselessness and futility.

When I meet with organizational leaders one-on-one, they often let their guard down and reveal a deep sense of discouragement with their efforts. It's rare for anyone in the organization to ask them about their feelings, so they take advantage of the opportunity to open up with me. Painfully, they say such things as:

"I had such high expectations when I came here, but all I've done is put out one fire after the next."

"I can't think of one thing I've done that's made a bit of difference."

"Every idea I propose gets shot down."

"All I've had is one disappointment after the next. I'm not sure how much more of this I can take."

What people who make statements such as these are really saying is that they've lost their sense of purpose. To a large extent, their future effectiveness depends on their ability to get this back.

Respect (Personal Character)

People need to view themselves as integrated (self-respect) and be viewed by others as being ethical and honest. Maslow includes respect as one of our ego needs. Other writers talk about our need for dignity. Respect is personal in focus because the emphasis is on one's character, which speaks to the question, "What kind of a person am I?" The perception of being regarded as someone with high ethical standards produces a feeling of inner peace, increasing one's sense of worth, while the perception of being regarded as someone with low ethical standards is a threat to one's sense of worth. Although people have a need for respect, they can also be motivated by a fear of being judged, causing them to become manipulative, defensively justify their actions, or engage in blame shifting.

In addition to competence, I'm struck by how quickly people judge each other's character in organizations. During one-on-one meetings, people often make such comments as the following:

"I wouldn't trust him with a ten foot pole."

"I always take what he says with a grain of salt."

"People warned me about her the day I was hired."

"We get along fine, but I wouldn't turn my back on him."

It's interesting to note that people who aren't trusted almost always perceive themselves as being worthy of trust. During one-on-one performance feedback sessions, when I tell people that others don't trust them, they're often shocked and react defensively, saying such things as, "I've never done anything to hurt them," or "Give me one example of a time when I was dishonest." The problem with trust issues is that people seldom bring them to the surface and deal with them directly. Unresolved trust issues can lie dormant for years, subtly affecting people's behavior toward each other, even if there's no evidence to support the mistrust. When I facilitate team building, getting people to surface and face these issues is high on my agenda, because I know they won't be able to accomplish much else unless they trust each other.

Acceptance (Social Character)

People need to see themselves as being viewed by others as worthy of acceptance. McClelland refers to this as the need for affiliation, while Maslow calls it the need for belonging. Acceptance focuses on ethics, because people usually believe including others is right, while excluding them is wrong. People can be members of a team in a formal sense but still not feel like others have accepted them. There are many reasons why people can feel rejected, including their physical appearance, personality, race, religion, socioeconomic status, seniority, values or beliefs. The perception of being accepted produces feelings of joy, happiness and contentment, adding to one's sense of self-worth, while the perception of being rejected produces feelings of hurt, lowering one's sense of self-worth. Although people have a need for acceptance, they can also be motivated by a fear of rejection, causing them to either hold back from others, or to become angry and lash out.

People become very discouraged when they don't feel accepted by others in an organization. This discouragement is revealed in such statements as the following:

"They ignore you unless you're not a member of the 'good-old-boy' club."

"The discrimination is very subtle, but I feel it all the time."

"They ask me how I'm doing, but they could care less."

Anything causing people to feel self-conscious, uneasy or excluded will have an inhibiting effect on their contribution to an organization. Instead of focusing on performance goals, they will be thinking about how awkward and uncomfortable they feel. In my experience, an atmosphere of acceptance and inclusiveness is absolutely essential to the development of an effective team or organization.

People function best when they care about the organization's purpose and vision, i.e. their personal purpose and vision are in line with those of the organization. And the more highly aligned the members of an organization are with each other as well as with the organization, the more effective they are likely to be.

Diagnosing & Dealing with Unmet Psychological Needs

A wide variety of negative behaviors in organizations, including resistance to change, are symptomatic of unmet psychological needs. Table 1.1 offers some examples of these symptoms, along with consequences of these symptoms and potential solutions. Two different kinds of symptoms can be distinguished: behaviors that people shouldn't engage in but do, and behaviors they should engage in but don't. The former might be called "sins of commission," such as showing up late to meetings and making derogatory comments about others behind their backs, while the latter could be referred to as "sins of omission," such as withholding help or failing to follow through on an agreed change.

There isn't a one-to-one relationship between a particular symptom and an underlying cause. Instead, symptoms should be viewed as data used to formulate hypotheses about causes. Thorough data collection allows for more accuracy in the diagnosis. Observing people's behavior and asking them to describe what others say and do that they find troubling can gather information about symptoms. As this is done, the data will start to form patterns pointing toward causes.

Table 1.1

Unmet Needs: Symptoms, Consequences, and Potential Solutions

Causes	Symptoms are that people:	Consequences	Potential Solutions
Unmet Need for *Mastery*	Expect too little from themselves. Lack opportunities to use their skills. Lack the necessary knowledge or understanding. Struggle to keep up with changes. Lack the required skill or ability. Avoid taking risks. Make too many mistakes. Have trouble staying on top of the job. Aren't encouraged to develop their skills. Make excuses for poor performance. Blame each other for mistakes. Have trouble getting enough work done. Have trouble with the quality of their work. Lack confidence in each other's ability. Create bottlenecks for others.	Low productivity Morale problems Complaints from customers Missed deadlines Cost overruns Layoffs Lost accounts Bankruptcy Frustration Resentment Fear of failure	Training Coaching/counseling Feedback Ask for help Offer to help each other Encourage others to do their best Empowerment Look for opportunities to use everyone's skills Expect everyone to do their very best Expect everyone to be responsible for their work
Unmet Need for *A Sense of Meaning & Purpose*	Disagree with the goals/methods of the team. Disagree with each other about priorities. Don't seem to care about their work. Feel treated like numbers, not persons. Feel their work goes unappreciated. Do the work because they have to, not because they want to. Lack a sense of accomplishment. Seem to lack motivation. Feel their work's unimportant. Don't feel their work contributes to the team. Feel their jobs are expendable. Feel unneeded by the team. Don't feel they receive enough recognition. Don't find their work very gratifying. Act like they're going through the motions.	Low productivity Morale problems Turnover Complaints Restlessness Poor reputation as a place to work Fear of purposelessness	Job enrichment Job rotation Cross-training Opportunities for advancement Career development program Meaningful incentives Empowerment Involvement Participation Express appreciation Give recognition Seek people's input Suggestion program

Causes	Symptoms are that people:	Consequences	Potential Solutions
Unmet Need for *Acceptance*	Judge each other on the basis of personal characteristics.	Low productivity	Convey that discrimination is unacceptable
	Discriminate against others.	Morale problems	Stress the benefits of diversity
	Subtly make others feel excluded.	Work environment perceived as hostile	Emphasize people's strengths
	Don't offer to help each other.		Team building
	Act superior to others.	Untapped talent	Diversity training
	Withhold constructive feedback.	Poor communication	Convey that team goals can't be accomplished without everyone's help
	Withhold encouragement/support.	Alienation, isolation	
	Just look out for themselves.	Self-consciousness	Seek input from everyone
	Reject those who are different.	Poor team/organization image	Remove barriers to full involvement and participation
	Form themselves into camps.	Lawsuits	Establish climate for open communication
	Have a "we-they" mentality.	Turnover	Confront problems directly
	Make new employees feel unwelcome.	Fear of rejection	
	Don't seem to value input from others.		
	Avoid each other.		
	Use favoritism to get what they want.		
Unmet Need for *Respect*	Malign each other's character.	Low productivity	Convey what behaviors are acceptable and unacceptable
	Withhold information from each other.	Morale problems	Establish a climate for open communication
	Try to make each other look bad.	Interpersonal conflict	Confront problems openly and directly
	Question each other's motives.	Lack of trust	
	Use manipulative tactics.	Poor communication	Nip problems in the bud
	Verbally attack each other.	Suspiciousness	Expect people to work out their differences
	Say one thing but do another.	Defensiveness	
	Say one thing to one person, something else to another person.	Posturing	Treat others the way you want to be treated
	Pretend to agree with each other.	Revenge/retaliation	
	Put each other down.	Poor team/organization image	Stress the importance of cooperation
	Start rumors about each other.	Polarization	
	Gossip about each other.	High level of tension	Refuse to listen to gossip
	Have hidden agendas.	Turnover	Hold people accountable for what they say and do
	Distort what others say.	Fear of judgment	
	Aren't honest with each other.		

Additional information can be collected by asking such questions as, "Does the team/organization make full use of your knowledge and skills?", "Do you feel your work makes a difference to the team/organization?", "Do you feel people treat you and each other with respect?", "Do you feel accepted by the team/organization?" Questions targeted to specific unmet needs often strike a responsive cord, because people are seldom asked about their feelings; their comments, therefore, are often quite candid and revealing.

A large number and diversity of symptoms indicates the presence of two, three, or even four unmet needs. In cases like this, it's important to determine which need represents the more serious problem.

Consequences refer to the negative results stemming from symptoms. Although every problem tends to bring about lower productivity and morale, additional consequences can often be traced back to specific unmet needs. Referring again to Table 1.1, some possible consequences of lack of respect are suspiciousness, defensiveness, and a poor team image. Observing the impact of team behavior, reviewing relevant performance data, and asking team members to describe the effects of their problems can gather information about consequences. Another useful approach is to seek input from outsiders who are impacted by people's behavior, such as internal and external customers, suppliers, and representatives from management. Often people either don't see or minimize the importance of their issues, so becoming aware that others perceive their behavior negatively can serve as an incentive for them to work toward solutions.

In dealing with organizational problems one of the most common mistakes is reacting to symptoms, instead of actively looking for solutions that deal with underlying needs. When this happens, it often makes the situation worse than it was before. If people show a lack of respect by verbally attacking each other, threatening them, for example, would only serve to increase defensiveness. It would be more constructive to have people generate a set of norms for how they want to be treated, and then come up with procedures for holding each other accountable when the norms are violated.

Facilitating Team Problem-Solving

When teams become polarized, it often takes the assistance of an internal or external consultant to help facilitate a process of positive change. By this time, team members are usually very defensive around each other and they're unable to look at their situation objectively, viewing everything from a win-lose perspective. Some members will even say they're convinced that change is impossible and they've given up trying.

No matter how serious a team's problems may be, the act of involving a consultant tends to instill hope, because it demonstrates that something's going to be done about the situation. When I work with troubled teams, I interview team members and some key people outside the team using a patterned interview format. I find that even the process of being interviewed starts to break down the polarity within the team, because people gain a broader perspective as they talk about relevant issues with someone who is willing to listen and not take sides. In addition, I gather additional information by administering the Psychological Need Fulfillment Inventory™. This instrument can be also used to assess organizational problems, but I have used it primarily with teams.

After all the data is collected, I prepare a written report organized into four categories: causes, symptoms, consequences, and potential solutions. Most of the information comes directly from the team members themselves. They can see the problems and have good ideas for solving them, but the polarity keeps them from cooperating toward solutions. As much as possible, I include direct quotes from team members, while making sure to maintain confidentiality. I find that this helps the team take ownership of the data. It's hard to argue with information when it's self-generated. The primary contribution I make is to organize the data in a way that provides the basis for a new synthesis.

The report is then distributed to all team members, who are given several days to review it and then attend a meeting to discuss the findings and develop a course of action. Between the time team members receive the report and come to the meeting, they will have had time to think about the results and discuss them informally among themselves.

I serve as facilitator at the meeting and start by thanking people for their honesty during the interviews. I review the psychological needs of people and state that unmet needs of team members have kept them from experiencing the advantages of having a team. I also reinforce the view that, regardless of how serious team problems may appear, the situation can be improved if everyone's willing to invest the necessary effort. Then I review the findings in the report and ask for questions. I'm particularly interested in knowing if they feel the information is accurate and complete.

The next step is for the team to agree upon a process for working on its issues. If lack of respect and/or acceptance have been identified as unmet needs, I suggest that the team focus on them first. Concerns in these areas are accompanied by the greatest amount of mistrust and interpersonal conflict, and progress here is usually necessary before people are willing to cooperate on other issues.

After the first meeting, they may want me to continue serving as facilitator or may elect to work on their own without my assistance. In either case, four conditions are essential to progress: (1) the team leader must clearly convey what behaviors are unacceptable among team members, (2) the emphasis during discussions should be on what team members are willing to do differently, rather than focusing on the past and blaming each other, (3) the solutions must relate directly to unmet needs, and not just be a reaction to symptoms, and (4) the people must be willing to honor agreements for change, because slipping back into old ways will result in more disillusionment than existed in the first place. If team members show a willingness to respond to each other's unmet needs, the tension and defensiveness will start to ease, and the team will become less polarized. In the beginning, even small changes are significant, because they demonstrate that things can be better. This is referred to as the "installation of hope." These initial signs of progress can provide the momentum necessary for the team to remove barriers to its effectiveness.

Summary

People are motivated to meet their various physical and psychological needs. The most important needs that people try to meet in the workplace are for mastery, a sense of meaning and purpose, respect and acceptance. These needs serve the larger purpose of helping people develop and maintain a sense of worth and value, which is crucial to their personal and interpersonal effectiveness. The Psychological Need Fulfillment Inventory™ can be used to assess the degree to which your team is meeting these needs currently.

PSYCHOLOGICAL NEED FULFILLMENT INVENTORY™

PURPOSE: To assess how effectively the organization is meeting your job-related psychological needs (60 items).

Procedure

Unmet psychological needs are responsible for many organizational problems, including interpersonal conflict and resistance to change. The Psychological Need Fulfillment Inventory™ is a behaviorally based instrument designed to assess how effectively a team or organization meets people's psychological needs. It can be used by itself to help identify the cause(s) of team or organizational problems, or in conjunction with other data-collection methods, such as the Change Opinion Survey™ and patterned interviews. It can also be used before and after an OD intervention to evaluate its effectiveness. If considerable tension exists among the people you plan to use it with, consider having them complete it anonymously. Avoid using both the Psychological Need Fulfillment Inventory™ and the Trust Scale with the same group of people, because there's an overlap of items. If you're trying to choose between the two, keep in mind that the former is more comprehensive, while the latter is specifically targeted to the issue of team trust. Before administering the Psychological Need Fulfillment Inventory™, specify whether a team or the organization is the focus of assessment.

Mean scores for the four psychological needs can vary from 0 to 60. The higher the mean score the better. A mean score below 20 indicate a serious problem.

One way to use the data is to display the completed Psychological Need Fulfillment Profile, and then facilitate a discussion of an organization/team's relative strengths and weaknesses in meeting needs. Calculating mean scores for individual items on the inventory, and then making a list of the lowest and highest items for each need can enhance this discussion. People are usually more candid in talking about negative behaviors once the data has been presented, because it represents a consensus regarding areas of concern.

Quite often inventory results contain some very low scores. While it's important to discuss these in depth, it's also important to focus on positive behaviors, because this provides a balanced view of organizational or team functioning. This helps instill a sense of hope that problems can be solved, while lowering the chances that people will become defensive.

Once problems have been identified, you can facilitate a discussion of possible solutions.

Psychological Need Fulfillment Inventory™

by
Ken Hultman

Name_____

Position_____

Team/Organization_____

Date Completed_____

Instructions

The Psychological Need Fulfillment Inventory™ is designed to assess the degree to which your team or organization is currently meeting people's job-related psychological needs. Organizations and teams that respond to the relevant needs of people can be expected to have higher morale and, therefore, be more productive. The scores will help identify strengths and areas where improvement is needed.

Read each item on the next two pages and circle the response that best describes your opinion. The scale is a continuum from 4 to 0, with 4 meaning strongly disagree and 0 meaning strongly agree. Your responses will be combined with those of others in your team and will be kept confidential. You will receive a summary of the results once they've been compiled.

THANK YOU FOR COMPLETING THIS INVENTORY

please turn the page and begin ⇒

	Strongly Disagree			Strongly Agree

People in my team/organization:

1.	Expect too little from themselves.	4	3	2	1	0
2.	Malign each other's character.	4	3	2	1	0
3.	Judge each other on the basis of personal characteristics.	4	3	2	1	0
4.	Disagree about goals/methods.	4	3	2	1	0
5.	Lack opportunities to use their skills.	4	3	2	1	0
6.	Withhold information from one another.	4	3	2	1	0
7.	Discriminate against others.	4	3	2	1	0
8.	Disagree with each other about priorities.	4	3	2	1	0
9.	Lack the necessary knowledge or understanding.	4	3	2	1	0
10.	Try to make each other look bad.	4	3	2	1	0
11.	Subtly make others feel excluded.	4	3	2	1	0
12.	Don't seem to care about their work.	4	3	2	1	0
13.	Struggle to keep up with changes.	4	3	2	1	0
14.	Question each other's motives.	4	3	2	1	0
15.	Don't offer to help each other.	4	3	2	1	0
16.	Feel treated like numbers, not persons.	4	3	2	1	0
17.	Lack the required skill or ability.	4	3	2	1	0
18.	Use manipulative tactics.	4	3	2	1	0
19.	Act superior to others.	4	3	2	1	0
20.	Feel their work goes unappreciated.	4	3	2	1	0
21.	Avoid taking risks.	4	3	2	1	0
22.	Verbally attack each other.	4	3	2	1	0
23.	Don't give each other enough constructive feedback.	4	3	2	1	0
24.	Do the work because they have to, not because they want to.	4	3	2	1	0
25.	Make too many mistakes.	4	3	2	1	0
26.	Say one thing but do another.	4	3	2	1	0
27.	Don't give each other enough encouragement or support.	4	3	2	1	0
28.	Lack a sense of accomplishment in their work.	4	3	2	1	0
29.	Have trouble staying on top of their job.	4	3	2	1	0
30.	Say one thing to one person, something else to another person.	4	3	2	1	0
31.	Just look out for themselves.	4	3	2	1	0

People in my team/organization:

		Strongly Disagree				Strongly Agree
32.	Seem to lack motivation.	4	3	2	1	0
33.	Aren't encouraged to develop their skills.	4	3	2	1	0
34.	Pretend to agree with each other.	4	3	2	1	0
35.	Form themselves into camps.	4	3	2	1	0
36.	Feel their work's unimportant.	4	3	2	1	0
37.	Make excuses for poor performance.	4	3	2	1	0
38.	Put each other down.	4	3	2	1	0
39.	Reject those who are different.	4	3	2	1	0
40.	Don't feel their work contributes very much.	4	3	2	1	0
41.	Blame each other for mistakes.	4	3	2	1	0
42.	Start rumors about each other.	4	3	2	1	0
43.	Have a "we-they" mentality.	4	3	2	1	0
44.	Feel their jobs are expendable.	4	3	2	1	0
45.	Have trouble getting enough work done.	4	3	2	1	0
46.	Gossip about each other.	4	3	2	1	0
47.	Make new employees feel unwelcome.	4	3	2	1	0
48.	Don't feel like they're needed.	4	3	2	1	0
49.	Have trouble with the quality of their work.	4	3	2	1	0
50.	Have hidden agendas.	4	3	2	1	0
51.	Don't seem to value input from others.	4	3	2	1	0
52.	Don't feel they receive enough recognition for their efforts.	4	3	2	1	0
53.	Lack confidence in each other's ability.	4	3	2	1	0
54.	Distort what others say.	4	3	2	1	0
55.	Avoid each other.	4	3	2	1	0
56.	Don't find their work very gratifying.	4	3	2	1	0
57.	Create bottlenecks for each other.	4	3	2	1	0
58.	Aren't honest with each other.	4	3	2	1	0
59.	Use favoritism to get what they want.	4	3	2	1	0
60.	Act like they're just going through the motions.	4	3	2	1	0

Calculating Scores

This instrument consists of 60 items, 15 pertaining to each of the psychological needs for mastery, respect, acceptance, and a sense of meaning and purpose. Following these procedures can develop a Psychological Need Fulfillment Profile:

1. Total up the scores of each team member for the four needs. Items pertaining to the needs are:

   Mastery: 1, 5, 9, 13, 17, 21, 25, 29, 33, 37, 41, 45, 49, 53, 57

   Respect: 2, 6, 10, 14, 18, 22, 26, 30, 34, 38, 42, 46, 50, 54, 58

   Acceptance: 3, 7, 11, 15, 19, 23, 27, 31, 35, 39, 43, 47, 51, 55, 59

   Meaning/Purpose: 4, 8, 12, 16, 20, 24, 28, 32, 36, 40, 44, 48, 52, 56, 60

2. Add the totals of all respondents together for each need, and divide these totals by the number of respondents completing the instrument. This will give you the mean or average scores for the four needs.

3. Place a dot at the corresponding point on the profile for each need, and connect the dots with a line.

Psychological Need Fulfillment Profile

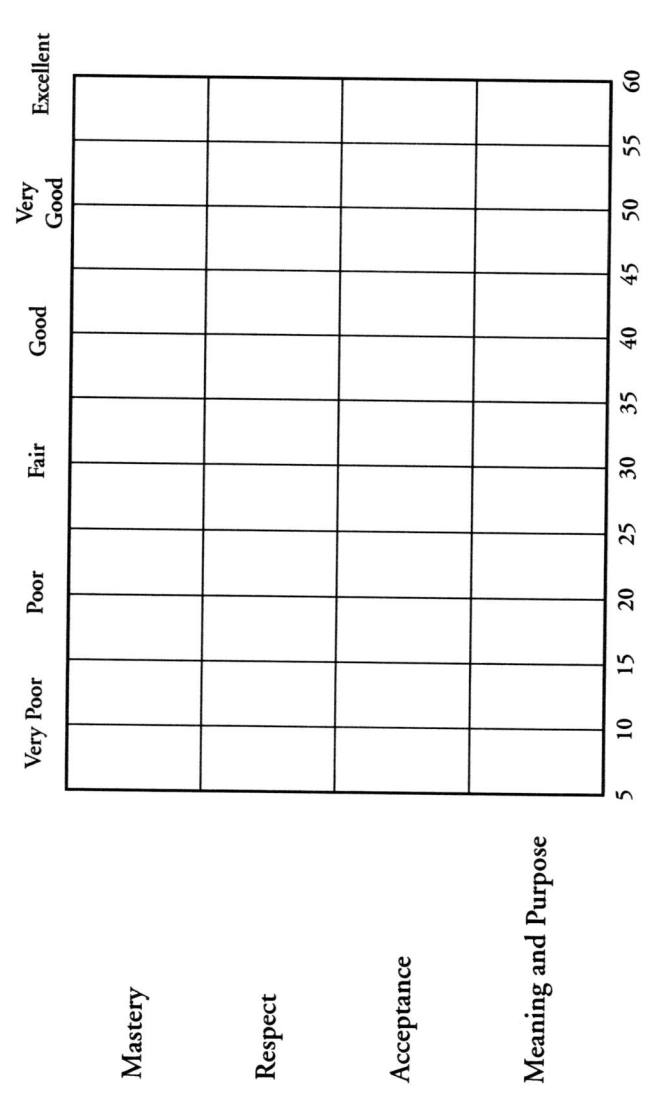

2

BUILDING TEAM TRUST

PURPOSE: To discuss the dynamics of trust and mistrust, provide a tool for assessing team trust, and a process for building it.

Introduction

When I work as a facilitator with teams experiencing interpersonal conflict, the members almost always tell me privately that they don't trust each other. Trust is a key factor contributing to team productivity, quality, morale and organizational growth; mistrust, on the other hand, saps the team of valuable time and energy, contributing to organizational suicide. The problem with mistrust is that it operates insidiously below the surface and, instead of dealing with it directly, people often build their work around it. With increasing competition, however, the assumption that mistrust can be tolerated is no longer viable. A basis for trust must be established if a team is to have any hope of developing its full potential. This chapter will shed some light on this important topic by (1) discussing the dynamics of trust and mistrust, (2) describing actions leading to mistrust, and (3) providing the Trust Scale and Plan for Building Trust, which can be used to assess and remove barriers to team trust.

The Dynamics of Trust

Trust can be defined as believing another person has your best interests at heart, whereas mistrust is believing that the other person doesn't have your best interests at heart. Mutual trust can be conceived as the condition that exists when parties to a relationship see one another as committed to seeking win-win (or all-win) results. Mistrust is a feeling the other person is trying to control or manipulate you to their end, rather than sharing control to accomplish some joint end. Trust is a dynamic variable that fluctuates up or down, depending on how we interpret another person's behavior. Thus, it's possible to trust someone to a greater extent one minute and less the next. We make adjustments like this on a conscious or subconscious basis all the time as we interact with other people.

Trust is an **output** that depends on certain *inputs*. In deciding whether or not to trust someone (the output), we evaluate his or her behavior according to its consistency and sincerity (the inputs). Consistency has to do with whether or not the other person is ethical, reliable, and dependable. The question we ask ourselves here is, *"Can I count on this person to do the right thing?"* Sincerity has to do with whether or not the other person is authentic and non-manipulative. The question we ask ourselves here is, *"Can I count on this person to really care about me?"* Consistency focuses on the predictability of the other person's observable

18

behavior. Sincerity focuses on the other person's motives, which can't be directly observed but must be inferred from their verbal and non-verbal behavior. Trust demands both consistency and sincerity; one without the other won't do. We not only need to believe the other person will do the right thing, but will do it for the right reasons. Figure 2.1 summarizes the effects of high and low levels of consistency and sincerity on trust.

Figure 2.1
Inputs for Trust

	High Consistency	Low Consistency
High Sincerity	High Trust	Mixed Message
Low Sincerity	Mixed Message	Low Trust

The condition of high consistency and high sincerity leads to trust, whereas the condition of low consistency and low sincerity leads to mistrust. The conditions of being consistent and insincere (*"He's doing the right thing but doesn't really care about us"*) and being inconsistent and sincere (*"She cares about us but doesn't follow through"*) send mixed messages that undermine trust.

Trust is such a crucial issue because we're aware that other people are capable of hurting us physically, emotionally and financially. In other words, relationships with other people involve risk, and we're careful not to take risks unless we believe it's safe to do so. Our behavior will vary tremendously depending on whether or not we trust the other person. Some of these differences are depicted in Figure 2.2.

In the Trust Pattern people are willing to make themselves vulnerable to another person, because they believe it's safe to do so. In the Mistrust Pattern, however, people spend their time protecting themselves from a situation they perceive as threatening. When people are in this mode, often they react in ways that cause others to mistrust them, creating a vicious cycle.

Research by Dale Zand (see Golembiewski, 1972) reported that in teams where high-trust conditions exist, there is:

- More open discussion of ideas and feelings.
- Greater clarification of goals and problems.
- A more thorough search for alternative courses of action.
- A greater sense of influence by all participants.

- More satisfaction with problem-solving efforts.
- A greater desire to implement decisions.
- A stronger feeling of team cohesiveness.

Results were the opposite in teams where low-trust conditions are present. Thus, it's very important to eliminate actions that lead to mistrust, and replace them with actions that build trust. The effort required to do this will be rewarded, because research has shown that a relationship exits between trust and bottom-line results. For example, Levering and Moskowitz (2000) found that shares of 58 publicly traded companies emphasizing such values as trust, pride, and camaraderie rose 37% annualized over the last three years, as compared to 25% for the S & P 500. Thus, increasing trust isn't just a nice thing to do; it's also good for business.

Figure 2.2
Patterns of Trust and Mistrust

Trust Pattern	Mistrust Pattern
Perception that the other person's behavior is consistent and sincere	Perception that the other person's behavior is inconsistent and/or insincere
← Conclusion that it's safe to trust	← Conclusion that it's **not** safe to trust
← Confidence	← Fear
← Willingness to take risks	**Fight** (Attack to deal with perceived danger) **Flight** (Escape or avoid perceived danger)

Actions Leading to Mistrust

A wide variety of actions can result in mistrust. Some of the more common examples are when team members:

- Say one thing but do another.
- Make agreements they don't keep.
- Say one thing to one person, something else to another person.
- Pretend to agree with others.
- Try to discredit others.

- Focus on other's mistakes.
- Withhold information.
- Make excuses for mistakes.
- Undercut others.
- Gossip about others.
- Play politics to get what they want.
- Form themselves into camps.
- Seek win-lose outcomes.
- Look out for their own interests.
- Use manipulative tactics.
- Make decisions affecting others without involving them.
- Put each other down.
- Blame others for mistakes.
- Have hidden agendas.
- Compete with each other.
- Try to get even with each other.
- Criticize each other.
- Have a "we-they" mentality.
- Openly attack each other.
- Give more negative feedback than positive.
- Spring surprises on others.
- Ignore input from others.
- Try to intimidate each other.
- Use information to their own advantage.
- Distort what people say.

Once trust has been violated it's difficult to restore, because people erect psychological barriers around their relationship with each other to protect themselves from getting hurt. Mistrust will continue indefinitely and become part of the corporate culture, unless people are willing to confront trust issues directly, eliminate actions contributing to mistrust, and engage in actions that will foster trust.

Suggestion for Enhancing Mutual Trust within a Team

Replacing the negative actions discussed above with more positive actions can increase mutual trust among team members. Some examples of such actions are as follows:

- Listen and convey understanding.
- Follow through on agreements.
- Resolve disagreements directly and in good faith.
- Say what you mean, mean what you say.
- Seek win-win outcomes.
- Be consistent in what you say to different people.
- Honor confidential information.
- Give others credit when it's due.
- Share information openly.
- Take responsibility for mistakes.
- Involve others in decisions affecting them.
- Avoid actions contributing to mistrust (gossip, blaming, etc.).
- Act out of integrity and not expediency.

Steps taken by teams to establish norms that encourage trust will help them become more successful, because energy currently being wasted fighting each other can be redirected toward more productive pursuits. The Trust Scale and Plan for Building Trust can be used to assess and remove barriers to team trust.

TRUST SCALE
AND
PLAN FOR BUILDING TRUST

PURPOSE: To assess the current level of team trust, and use the results to facilitate a team-building workshop (30 items).

This workbook allows you to facilitate a workshop on building team trust, which usually takes from 4 to 8 hours, depending upon the amount of interpersonal conflict existing in a team. In some cases, additional sessions will be required.

Specifically you can use the materials to (1) assess the current level of trust, (2) identify behaviors causing mistrust, and (3) develop a plan of action for building trust. The Trust Scale can be administered before and after the workshop to evaluate its effectiveness. Avoid using both the Psychological Need Fulfillment Inventory™ and the Team Trust Scale with the same group of people, because there's an overlap of items. If you're trying to choose between the two, keep in mind that the former is more comprehensive, while the latter is specifically targeted to the issue of team trust.

Procedure for the Trust Scale

Give a copy of the Trust Scale to people, and ask them to complete it anonymously and return it to you on a specified date.

The Trust Scale consists of 30 items describing behaviors contributing to mistrust. When you receive back all of the completed instruments, add the scores for all team members together to get a total score, and then divide the total score by the number of respondents to get the team's mean score.

Next, mark the spot on the Trust Profile representing the team's mean score. Make enough copies of the completed profile to give to each team member at the workshop, and make an overhead transparency or computer slide of the profile that you can display.

Finally, go back over the completed instruments and identify the 5-10 items receiving the lowest scores. Place these items on a sheet of paper in rank order (lowest item first). Entitle the sheet "Behaviors Most Contributing to Mistrust" and make enough copies for each member.

At the beginning of the workshop, after the introductions and perhaps reviewing some of the key points about trust and mistrust, do the following:

- HAND OUT a copy of the completed Trust Profile to each team member, while displaying the overhead transparency you prepared.

- EXPLAIN how to interpret the results:
The lower the score, the more mistrust that exists in a team. Scores from 0 to 60 indicate that mistrust is an issue in your team. The lower your score **below** 60, the more likely it is that mistrust could be preventing the team from achieving its objectives.

- ASK for and RESPOND to questions.

Procedures for the Mistrust Identification Exercise

- HAND OUT the sheet you prepared ahead of time entitled "Behaviors Most Contributing to Mistrust."

- REVIEW the items with the team.

- FACILITATE a discussion of these items, in an effort to promote greater understanding of team behaviors causing mistrust (this discussion may be short or long, depending on the specific issues).

Procedure for the Plan for Building Trust

After you're done facilitating the Team Mistrust Identification Exercise it's time to focus on solutions, by helping the team develop a Plan for Building Trust.

- EXPLAIN the purpose of developing an action plan:
This is an opportunity to pull together information gathered from the *Team Trust Scale* and the discussion of team behaviors causing mistrust, to decide what actions you can take to build trust and eliminate mistrust.

- HAND OUT a copy of the two page Plan for Building Trust to each team member.

- GIVE instructions for completing the Plan for Building Trust:
Individually, take about 15 minutes to identify what you can do to make it easier for others to trust you, and list these ideas in the first box. Please be specific about what you will do and when.

Then meet with your team to discuss what you can do to improve trust (1) within the team, (2) with other teams, (3) with upper management, and (4) with others (customers, suppliers distributors, the union, employees, etc.). Use the remainder of the first page and the second page to jot down notes from your team discussion.

- FACILITATE this discussion, listing the team's agreements for action on a flip chart.

- ASK for a volunteer who will agree to have the flip charts typed and distributed to each team member.

- ASK the team to agree on a plan for following up on the agreements made for building trust.

- SUMMARIZE key outcomes from this workshop and COMPLIMENT the team for its hard work.

Trust Scale

by
Ken Hultman

TEAM: _____   DATE: _____

Please read each item and circle the response that best reflects your opinion.

	Almost Never				Almost Always

The people in my team:

1.	Say one thing but do another.	4	3	2	1	0
2.	Make agreements they don't keep.	4	3	2	1	0
3.	Say one thing to one person, something else to another person.	4	3	2	1	0
4.	Pretend to agree with others.	4	3	2	1	0
5.	Try to discredit others.	4	3	2	1	0
6.	Focus on other's mistakes.	4	3	2	1	0
7.	Withhold information.	4	3	2	1	0
8.	Make excuses for mistakes.	4	3	2	1	0
9.	Undercut others.	4	3	2	1	0
10.	Gossip about others.	4	3	2	1	0
11.	Play politics to get what they want.	4	3	2	1	0
12.	Form themselves into camps.	4	3	2	1	0
13.	Seek win-lose outcomes.	4	3	2	1	0
14.	Look out for their own interests.	4	3	2	1	0
15.	Use manipulative tactics.	4	3	2	1	0
16.	Make decisions affecting others without involving them.	4	3	2	1	0
17.	Put each other down.	4	3	2	1	0
18.	Blame others for mistakes.	4	3	2	1	0
19.	Have hidden agendas.	4	3	2	1	0
20.	Compete with each other.	4	3	2	1	0
21.	Try to get even with each other.	4	3	2	1	0
22.	Criticize each other.	4	3	2	1	0
23.	Have a "we-they" mentality.	4	3	2	1	0

	Almost Never		Almost Always

The people in my team:

24.	Openly attack each other.	4	3	2	1	0
25.	Give more negative feedback than positive.	4	3	2	1	0
26.	Spring surprises on others.	4	3	2	1	0
27.	Ignore input from others.	4	3	2	1	0
28.	Try to intimidate each other.	4	3	2	1	0
29.	Use information to their own advantage.	4	3	2	1	0
30.	Distort what people say.	4	3	2	1	0

TOTAL SCORE: _____

Trust Profile

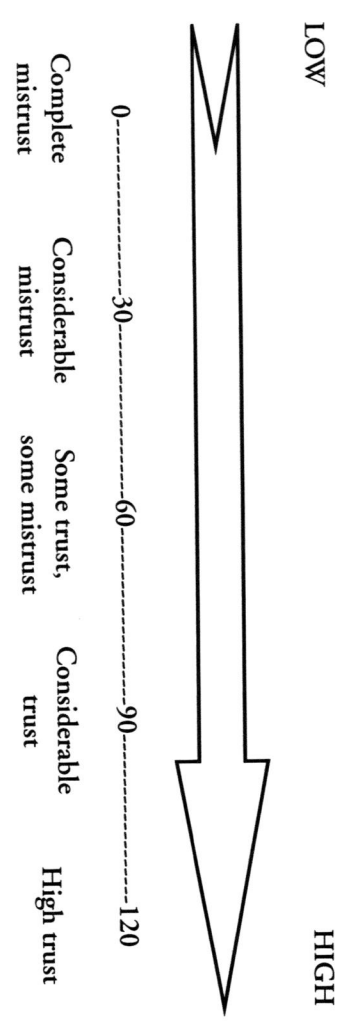

LOW

HIGH

0 --------- 30 --------- 60 --------- 90 --------- 120

Complete
mistrust

Considerable
mistrust

Some trust,
some mistrust

Considerable
trust

High trust

Plan for Building Trust

1. What I can do to make it easier for others to trust me.

WHAT _____   WHEN

2. What we can do to improve trust within our team

WHAT _____   WHEN

3. What we can do to improve trust with other teams.

WHAT

WHEN
_____

4. What we can do to improve trust with upper management

WHAT

WHEN
_____

5. What we can do to improve trust with others
(customers, suppliers, distributors, the union, employees, community.)

WHAT

WHEN
_____

PART 2

VALVES-DRIVEN PERSONAL CHANGE

3. Removing Barriers to Peak Performance

   Offers a framework for understanding the causes of performance problems, and the Peak Performance Inventory™, which can be used to identify the causes of performance problems. Also includes exercises for establishing a personal vision, building self-worth and doing a values-driven life reassessment.

4. Becoming a New Paradigm Thinker in the Global Economy

   Describes the mindset required for success in the global economy, and provides the Mega-Value Scale™ and Plan for Personal Change, which can be used for self-assessment and personal change.

3

REMOVING BARRIERS TO PEAK PERFORMANCE

PURPOSE: To provide a framework for understanding the causes of performance problems, a tool for assessing barriers to peak performance, and exercises for building self-esteem, establishing a personal vision, and doing a values-driven life reassessment.

Introduction

In any given situation, the performance of an individual is a function of at least four variables: Commitment, Confidence, Competence, and Contingencies.[1] Contingencies are subdivided into Working Conditions and Communication. Each variable will now be discussed in detail. This discussion can also be used to interpret results from the Peak Performance Inventory™, included at the end of the chapter.

Commitment

Commitment has to do with values, your beliefs about what's important in life. Values are the criteria we use to evaluate alternatives, and they allow us to set priorities. Without values, decision-making would be impossible. A high score on commitment indicates that your priorities, interests and goals are in tune with those of the organization. This allows you to have a sense of pride in your place of employment. It also gives you a feeling of belonging, and a desire to do your best. In contrast, a low score on commitment indicates that conflict exists between your values and those of the organization. In all likelihood, you have trouble identifying with the goals and/or methods of the organization, feel alienated from others on the job, and dream about working elsewhere. Unless the specific reasons for your value conflict can be identified and changed, it's unlikely that you will be motivated to achieve your potential.

Confidence

Confidence refers to *perceived* ability, or what you believe you can do. Confidence, or the lack of it, is a powerful determinant of performance. People who see themselves as inadequate tend to behave consistently with this belief, even if there's no rational basis for it. A high score on confidence indicates that you believe you can do the job, while a low score means you doubt your ability, worry about how others view you, and

---

1   These concepts were fist presented in my article, "The psychology of performance management," *Training and Development Journal*, 42 (7), 1988. © 1989, Kenneth E. Hultman. All rights reserved.

avoid taking risks. To improve your performance, it's important to bring your beliefs about your abilities into alignment with your actual abilities. This means identifying and getting rid of any inaccurate beliefs that may be holding you back. Coaching or counseling is often a useful way to facilitate this process.

Competence

Competence is actual ability. In contrast to commitment and confidence, which are internal to a person and cannot be observed directly, competence relates to what a person does. While commitment and confidence can be faked, you can't pretend to be competent. In measuring competence, the bottom line is simple: you can do a task, you can be trained to do it, or you cannot or will not do it. A high score on competence indicates that you are able to carry out your tasks both effectively and efficiently, while a low score means you're struggling to meet your performance expectations. It's important to identify the reasons for a low score on competence so you can take corrective actions. Sometimes additional training is indicated, while at other times a job change is in order.

Contingencies

Contingencies are factors in the work environment that impact performance. As with competence, specific contingencies are present or absent in varying degrees. Favorable contingencies foster performance, while unfavorable contingencies detract from one's willingness and ability to do the job. Contingencies can be sub-divided into two categories: Conditions of Work and Communication.

- **Working Conditions.** Conditions of work are largely concerned with the availability and allocation of material and human resources, such as staff, money, time, equipment, supplies and training. Also included are items pertaining to the terms of your employment, such as pay, performance standards, and authority to match responsibility. A high score indicates that your working conditions are favorable, which should help you perform up to your capabilities. In contrast, a low score means your working conditions are unfavorable, which will have a negative impact on your output. Poor working conditions need to be identified and eliminated, so they aren't blocking your efforts to do the job.

- **Communication.** Communication has to do with the interpersonal environment on the job, and concerns such issues as the amount of supervision, feedback, encouragement, cooperation, support and information you receive. Also included here are the extent to which you trust your co-workers, and feel included when decisions affecting you are being made. A high score indicates that communication within the organization fosters your performance, while a low score means it interferes with your ability to do the job. People need to work together to resolve communication problems, so they don't interfere with performance.

Separating Symptoms from Causes of Performance Problems

Any one of the four performance variables could be either a symptom or cause of problems with other variables. One useful way of distinguishing causes from symptoms is to look at performance as a set of inputs and outputs. If commitment, confidence, competence, and contingencies are inputs, then feelings and behaviors are outputs. Outputs vary for each input and either encourage or discourage a person's performance. Labeling specific discouraging feelings and behaviors can help identify those inputs causing problems. The inputs and outputs of performance are summarized in Figure 3.1. If you experience any of the discouraging feelings and/or behaviors associated with a particular input that could be a cause of your struggle.

Another approach is to ask yourself, "What's keeping me from working up to my potential? Is it that I don't want to do the work (commitment); I don't expect to do well (confidence); I lack the knowledge and/or skills (competence); or that conditions within the work environment get in the way (contingencies)?"

Figure 3.1
The Inputs and Outputs of Performance

INPUTS	OUTPUTS	
	FEELINGS	BEHAVIORS
COMMITMENT		
• High: *"I want to do this."*	Inner harmony, a sense of rightness, determination, peace of mind, a sense of purpose, enthusiasm	Willing to do the best job possible.
• Low: *"I don't want to do this."*	Inner conflict, confusion, restlessness, emptiness, purposelessness, boredom	Willing only to do the minimum to get by.
CONFIDENCE		
• Rational Beliefs: *"I can do this."*	Inner assurance, optimism	Logical, reasonable, positive self-talk
• Irrational Beliefs: *"I can't do this."*	Uncertainty, pessimism, fear of exposure, criticism, failure, rejection, judgment	Illogical, unreasonable, negative self-talk

INPUTS

	OUTPUTS	
	FEELINGS	**BEHAVIORS**
COMPETENCE		
• Present: *"I did it."*	Pride, satisfaction, fulfillment, elation, joy, happiness, pleasure	Successful: performs effectively; keeps trying
• Absent: *"I didn't do it."*	Shame, regret, remorse, humiliation, envy, jealousy, embarrassment	Unsuccessful: performs ineffectively; gives up or doesn't try
CONTINGENCIES		
• Favorable: *"They'll give me what I need to do it."*	Gratitude, trust, belonging, loyalty	Supportive: helps by cooperating sharing, forgiving, accepting
• Unfavorable: *"They won't give me what I need to do it."*	Anger, bitterness, resentment, frustration, hurt, suspicion, alienation	Divisive: gets even by competing, resisting, criticizing, blaming, retaliating, sabotaging

Performance Improvement Tools

The Peak Performance Inventory™ can be used to identify why you might not be working up to your full potential. After completing the instrument, the Performance Improvement Worksheet can be used to develop a plan of action. Sometimes people don't work up to their potential because they lack a personal vision. The Personal Vision Exercise is included to facilitate this process. Others don't work up to their potential because of low self-esteem. The Self-Worth Exercise is included to help identify and work through self-esteem issues. Finally, sometimes people benefit from taking a more comprehensive look at their life before addressing specific performance issues. The Values-Driven Life Reassessment can be used for this purpose.

PEAK PERFORMANCE INVENTORY™

by
Ken Hultman

Instructions

The inventory consists of 75 items. Review each item and circle the response that best applies to you. Then calculate your scores, place them on the Peak Performance Profile, and connect the dots with a line. Finally, read the Interpretation section and complete the Performance Improvement Worksheet.

		Almost Never				Almost Always
1.	I resist giving my best effort.	4	3	2	1	0
2.	I dwell on past failures.	4	3	2	1	0
3.	I expect too much of myself.	4	3	2	1	0
4.	People I work with are unreliable.	4	3	2	1	0
5.	I have conflict with co-workers.	4	3	2	1	0
6.	I disagree with organizational goals/methods.	4	3	2	1	0
7.	I'm unsure of myself.	4	3	2	1	0
8.	I feel like I'd be better at a different job.	4	3	2	1	0
9.	I feel like I need more training.	4	3	2	1	0
10.	I lack adequate supervision.	4	3	2	1	0
11.	I find my work unfulfilling.	4	3	2	1	0
12.	I feel intimidated by others.	4	3	2	1	0
13.	I have trouble staying on top of the job.	4	3	2	1	0
14.	I lack adequate space.	4	3	2	1	0
15.	I mistrust people I work with.	4	3	2	1	0
16.	I disagree with co-workers about priorities.	4	3	2	1	0
17.	I become easily discouraged.	4	3	2	1	0
18.	I lack the necessary knowledge/understanding.	4	3	2	1	0
19.	Work deadlines are unrealistic.	4	3	2	1	0
20.	Co-workers show a lack of respect toward me.	4	3	2	1	0
21.	I feel what I'm doing is unimportant.	4	3	2	1	0
22.	I feel less capable than others.	4	3	2	1	0
23.	I struggle to keep up with changes.	4	3	2	1	0
24.	The standards for output keep changing.	4	3	2	1	0
25.	I feel left out when decisions are being made.	4	3	2	1	0
26.	I dread going to work.	4	3	2	1	0
27.	I'm concerned about losing my job.	4	3	2	1	0
28.	I put things off until the last minute.	4	3	2	1	0
29.	Mistakes made by others disrupt my work.	4	3	2	1	0
30.	Work expectations are unclear.	4	3	2	1	0
31.	I dream about doing a different type of work.	4	3	2	1	0
32.	I worry about being criticized.	4	3	2	1	0
33.	I lack the required skill or ability.	4	3	2	1	0

	Almost Never				Almost Always

34.	I'm given work that isn't in my job description.	4	3	2	1	0
35.	I feel treated like a number, not a person.	4	3	2	1	0
36.	I feel restless at work.	4	3	2	1	0
37.	I avoid taking risks.	4	3	2	1	0
38.	I feel burned out.	4	3	2	1	0
39.	I have inadequate ventilation/lighting.	4	3	2	1	0
40.	I feel my work goes unappreciated.	4	3	2	1	0
41.	I do only the minimum to get by.	4	3	2	1	0
42.	I feel self-conscious at work.	4	3	2	1	0
43.	I take too much time to complete tasks.	4	3	2	1	0
44.	The expectations to produce are too high.	4	3	2	1	0
45.	Complaining by co-workers disturbs my work.	4	3	2	1	0
46.	I only do the work because I have to.	4	3	2	1	0
47.	I question whether I could ever improve.	4	3	2	1	0
48.	I have trouble staying within my budget.	4	3	2	1	0
49.	I lack the necessary materials/supplies.	4	3	2	1	0
50.	Lack of information impairs my work.	4	3	2	1	0
51.	I rush through, just to get done.	4	3	2	1	0
52.	I worry about making mistakes.	4	3	2	1	0
53.	Some of the tasks are too difficult.	4	3	2	1	0
54.	My budget is too small to do the job right.	4	3	2	1	0
55.	My work is hindered by interruptions.	4	3	2	1	0
56.	I feel out of place in the job/organization.	4	3	2	1	0
57.	I expect to do poorly.	4	3	2	1	0
58.	I have problems with the quality of my work.	4	3	2	1	0
59.	I feel underpaid for what I do.	4	3	2	1	0
60.	Cooperation between people is lacking.	4	3	2	1	0
61.	I have trouble deciding what I want to do.	4	3	2	1	0
62.	I worry about what others think of me.	4	3	2	1	0
63.	I make too many mistakes.	4	3	2	1	0
64.	I have fewer staff than necessary.	4	3	2	1	0
65.	I feel like I'm treated unfairly.	4	3	2	1	0
66.	I lack enthusiasm for my work.	4	3	2	1	0

	Almost Never			Almost Always
67. I tell myself I can't do the work.	4	3	2	1	0
68. I have trouble getting enough work done.	4	3	2	1	0
69. I lack the necessary authority.	4	3	2	1	0
70. I lack constructive feedback from others.	4	3	2	1	0
71. I have trouble balancing my priorities.	4	3	2	1	0
72. I worry about being embarrassed/humiliated.	4	3	2	1	0
73. Even my best effort seems inadequate.	4	3	2	1	0
74. I lack the necessary equipment.	4	3	2	1	0
75. I lack encouragement/support from others.	4	3	2	1	0

Calculating Scores

Add up the scores you gave yourself for the 15 items pertaining to each of the four performance factors: **Commitment**, **Confidence**, **Competence**, and **Contingencies**. Contingencies are sub-divided into **Working Conditions and Communication**.

			Contingencies	
Commitment	Confidence	Competence	Working Conditions	Communication
1. ___	2. ___	3. ___	4. ___	5. ___
6. ___	7. ___	8. ___	9. ___	10. ___
11. ___	12. ___	13. ___	14. ___	15. ___
16. ___	17. ___	18. ___	19. ___	20. ___
21. ___	22. ___	23. ___	24. ___	25. ___
26. ___	27. ___	28. ___	29. ___	30. ___
31. ___	32. ___	33. ___	34. ___	35. ___
36. ___	37. ___	38. ___	39. ___	40. ___
41. ___	42. ___	43. ___	44. ___	45. ___
46. ___	47. ___	48. ___	49. ___	50. ___
51. ___	52. ___	53. ___	54. ___	55. ___
56. ___	57. ___	58. ___	59. ___	60. ___
61. ___	62. ___	62. ___	63. ___	65. ___
66. ___	67. ___	68. ___	69. ___	70. ___
71. ___	72. ___	73. ___	74. ___	75. ___

TOTALS: ___ ___ ___ ___ ___

Peak Performance Profile

Place a dot next to your scores on the Profile, and connect the dots with a line.

	Very Poor	Poor	Fair	Good	Very Good	Excellent
Commitment						
Confidence						
Competence						
Working Conditions						
Communication						
MEAN SCORES:	0 5 10	15 20	25 30	35 40	45 50	55 60

Interpretation

Peak performance can be expected if scores for all four variables are high (above 40), while low scores (below 30) on one or more variables can keep you from working up to your potential. If you received a low score on more than one performance variable, it will be necessary for you to separate causes from symptoms. The reason many performance improvements efforts fail is that they respond to symptoms instead of causes. Dealing with causes takes care of the symptoms, while dealing with symptoms only leads to frustration, discouragement, and lower performance levels.

Performance Improvement Worksheet

After identifying the cause(s) of your performance problems, complete the Performance Improvement Worksheet by following these steps:

1. List the cause(s) in column one.

2. For each cause identified, set goal(s) for performance improvement in column two.

3. Indicate specific actions you will take to achieve each goal in column three.

4. Specify how and when you will measure progress toward achieving each goal in column four.

Performance Improvement Worksheet

1. List the cause(s) of your performance problems.	2. For each cause, set goals for improvement.	3. Indicate specific actions you will take to achieve each goal.	4. Specify how and when you will measure results of actions taken.	
			<u>How</u>	<u>When</u>

PERSONAL VISION EXERCISE

PURPOSE: To help individual's clarify their personal vision or dreams for the future, and then take steps to fulfill that vision. It is designed to take two hours.

Procedures for Group use

1. **SAY**, "We all have dreams, fantasies, wishes and hopes about things we'd like our lives to fulfill, but for one reason or another we end up not doing what it takes to bring them into being."

2. **ASK**, "What are some of the reasons we don't follow our dreams?"

3. **LIST** participant responses on an easel, making sure to include the following reasons:

   Lack of time

   Lack of money

   Procrastination

   Laziness

   Dismiss them as unrealistic

   Lack of self-confidence

   Fear of failure

   Fear of criticism or disapproval

   Settling for someone else's vision

4. **SAY**, "Regardless of whatever else is going on in our lives, our dreams and fantasies keep tugging at us. The reason is that our dreams are part of who we are as persons. Therefore, neglecting our dreams prevents us from being true to ourselves. Today I'm going to challenge you to develop your dreams into a personal vision for the future, and then to think of ways you can start making your vision a reality,"

5. **DIVIDE** participants into groups of four.

6. **HAND OUT** a copy of the pages entitled Coaching Questions and Personal Vision Worksheet to each participant and **GIVE** the following instructions:

   "Take a few minutes to complete the Personal Vision Worksheet individually."

   "Then each person takes turns being a Presenter and a Coach. While in the Presenter role, the information you placed on the Personal Vision Worksheet will be the focus of group attention.

The Coach will ask you a series of questions designed to clarify your vision and the steps required to achieve it."

"The coaching questions are designed to encourage risk-taking and self-disclosure, by allowing the Presenter to learn through self-discovery in a setting free from evaluation and interpretation."

7. **DEBRIEF** key learning points with the full group by asking these questions:

"Who would like to share their personal vision for the future?"

"What ideas did you generate for making your vision a reality?"

"What impact has this exercise had on your views about who you are as persons?"

8. **ASK** for and **RESPOND** to questions.

Procedures for Individual use

1. Think about your dreams and fantasies for the future.

2. Answer the questions on the Personal Vision Worksheet page, making sure to identify specific actions you can take to start bringing your vision into reality.

Coaching Questions

1. What is your personal vision for the future? What would your life be like if it were exactly the way you wanted it to be? [Think about yourself, your family and friends, your work, your community, the world, and any other things you think about in relation to this question.]

2. Do you have any beliefs about yourself, other people, or your situation that keep you from following your vision?

3. How did these beliefs originate?

4. Are these beliefs valid currently? If so, what evidence do you have?

5. What would have to change in order for you to follow your vision?

6. How could you go about making these changes?

7. What risks are involved? How could these risks be eliminated?

8. What's the very first step you could take to make your vision a reality?

9. When could you take this step?

10. What will you do if you don't succeed? Do you have a back-up plan?

Personal Vision Worksheet

What is your personal vision for the future?	What steps can you take to move toward bringing your vision into reality?

SELF-WORTH EXERCISE

PURPOSE: To help people achieve a greater degree of self-worth and self-acceptance, so they're freer psychologically to pursue values emphasizing growth and development. It is designed to take two hours.

Procedures for Group Use

1. PLACE the following continuum on an easel:

Completely
Conditional

Completely
Unconditional

2. COVER the following points:

"Our sense of self-worth has a tremendous impact on both our choices and behavior. Self-worth, which consists of all the beliefs we hold about ourselves as persons, can be placed on a continuum extending from completely conditional to completely unconditional."

"People at the conditional end of the continuum base their self-worth on performance and/or personal characteristics, so it rises and falls with their successes and failures. They're constantly trying to prove their worth by striving for recognition, approval, success, and material possessions. Since failure and rejection are always possibilities, however, they're frequently fearful and defensive."

"In contrast, people at the unconditional end of the continuum keep their self-worth separate from their performance and/or personal characteristics, so it remains steady independent of situations. They accept themselves in spite of their weaknesses and limitations. Instead of using judgmental terms like success and failure they focus on learning, and use their talents and abilities to express who they are as persons."

"Self-worth is not static, but changes as we go through life. While children are born with unconditional self-acceptance, through the process of socialization they soon link their worth as persons to what significant others regard as important: physical attractiveness, school grades, special talents, popularity, excelling in sports, being dutiful and compliant, etc."

"As people mature they tend to move from an external to a more internal locus of self-evaluation, but many continue to be held back by unfavorable social comparisons and by the perception that they are less worthy than others. For example, when people make mistakes it is commonplace to hear them say such things as, "I never do anything right," or "I feel so worthless." It's important to identify and eliminate negative beliefs about self that keep one's worth conditional, because these serve as barriers to growth and development."

3. **DIVIDE** participants into groups of four.

4. **HAND OUT** a copy of the pages entitled Coaching Questions and Self-Worth Worksheet to each participant and **GIVE** the following instructions:

"Take a few minutes to complete the Self-Worth Worksheet individually.

"Then each person should take turns being a Presenter and a Coach. While in the Presenter role, the information you placed on the Self-Worth Worksheet will be the focus of group attention. The Coach will ask you a series of questions designed to clarify your beliefs about yourself and to help you achieve greater self-acceptance."

"The coaching questions are designed to encourage risk-taking and self-disclosure, by allowing the Presenter to learn through self-discovery in a setting free from evaluation and interpretation."

5. **DEBRIEF** key learning points with the full group by asking these questions:
"What did you learn about yourselves during the small-group discussion?"

"What ideas did you generate for achieving greater self-acceptance?"

"In what ways do you think greater self-acceptance can help you in the future?"

6. **ASK** for and **RESPOND** to questions.

Procedures for Individual use

1. Think about how your childhood experiences shaped your sense of self-worth, and how this has changed over the years.

2. Answer the questions on the Self-Worth Worksheet page, making sure to identify specific actions you can take to gain a greater degree of self-acceptance.

Coaching Questions

1. What beliefs do you have about yourself as a person?

2. How did these beliefs originate?

3. What impact did these beliefs have on you as a child?

4. How do these beliefs affect you now?

5. How can you develop greater feelings of self-worth and self-acceptance?

Self-Worth Worksheet

What beliefs do you have about yourself?	How did these beliefs originate?	What impact do these beliefs have on your life?	What can you do to develop greater feelings of self-worth and self-acceptance?

VALUES-DRIVEN LIFE REASSESSMENT

PURPOSE: To compare how your daily activities relate to your values, and to increase the amount of time you spend in valued activities.

Our choices in life are based on how we answer two key questions: What do I *want* to do, and what do I *have* to do? What we want to do pertains to our values, i.e. what's important to us; what we have to do pertains to our responsibilities or obligations. If you take the two questions together you can categorize everything you do into four domains:

1. Things I want to do *and* have to do (Domain of *responsibility*)

2. Things I want to do *but* don't have to do (Domain of *freedom*)

3. Things I don't want to do *but* believe I have to do (Domain of *obligation*)

4. Things I neither want to do nor have to do (Domain of *indifference*)

The Values-Driven Life Reassessment is an opportunity to reassess how you spend your time. Here's the challenge: if a lot of your time is taken up with things in the Domain of Obligation, you will feel trapped and unfulfilled. You can enrich your life by identifying and eliminating as many of these things as possible, and investing more of your energy in the Domain of Responsibility, and the Domain of Freedom.

Some further clarification regarding the Domain of Responsibility might be useful. Taking on responsibility is necessary for people to develop emotional maturity; people who don't take on responsibility tend to remain self-centered and emotionally immature. At the same time, taking on responsibility means giving up some personal freedom. If the responsibility is accepted willingly, it can give you a sense of meaning and purpose; if responsibility isn't accepted willingly, however, it will cause internal conflict. You will feel trapped by the responsibility and carry it out begrudgingly. In addition, assuming responsibility is dynamic: it can be accepted willingly at one point but become an unwanted burden at another. In either case it's important to assess whether the responsibility is something you actually *have* to do. Sometimes people believe they have to do things, but on closer inspection they come to see that they don't.

Similarly, people often confuse what they want to do with what they *should* do. They say they want to do something, but they actually believe they should do it. There's nothing wrong with basing your actions on a sense of duty or on specific moral beliefs, but many shoulds, oughts, and musts are based on other people's expectations and only serve to reduce freedom of choice. Therefore it's important to examine the basis for the things you say you want to do, to ensure that they have validity for your current life.

On the CURRENT Values-Driven Life Assessment form, think about the things that fill your life now and place them in the appropriate domains. Then on the DESIRED Values-Driven Life Assessment form, indicate changes or additions you'd like to make. List the possibilities that come to mind without evaluating them; there will be time for that later. Finally develop a plan for making the desired changes, indicating specifically what you plan to do and by when. Remember, it's your life; you're empowered to make it what you want.

Values-Driven Life Reassessment

CURRENT

	Things I Have To Do	Things I Don't Have To Do
Things I Want To Do	1. Things I want to do *and* have to do (Domain of *responsibility*)	2. Things I want to do *but* don't have to do (Domain of *freedom*)
Things I Don't Want To Do	3. Things I don't want to do *but* believe I have to do (Domain of *obligation*)	4. Things I neither want to do nor have to do (Domain of *indifference*)

Values-Driven Life Reassessment

DESIRED

	Things I Have To Do	Things I Don't Have To Do
Things I Want To Do	1. Things I want to do *and* have to do (Domain of *responsibility*)	2. Things I want to do *but* don't have to do (Domain of *freedom*)
Things I Don't Want To Do	3. Things I don't want to do *but* believe I have to do (Domain of *obligation*)	4. Things I neither want to do nor have to do (Domain of *indifference*)

Moving Toward the Life I Want

What I Plan To Do	By When

4

BECOMING A NEW PARADIGM THINKER IN THE GLOBAL ECONOMY

PURPOSE: To describe the mindset required for success in the global economy, and to provide tools for self-assessment and personal change.

Introduction

A paradigm is a model or way of thinking that explains how something works. A "paradigm shift" occurs when generally accepted facts, beliefs, values and behaviors no longer allow people to meet their needs—like a road map that doesn't get you where you want to go. The trend toward a global economy represents a paradigm shift, a whole new way of thinking about how business is conducted. Throughout history there have been many paradigm shifts, and there will be others in the future. Globalization of the marketplace is the *current* paradigm shift, the one with which we are confronted at this point in time. Using the metaphor of rafting on a river, Peter Vaill (1996) refers to this as *permanent white water*. In response to this, each of us is required to make our own personal paradigm shift if we hope to be successful in navigating the flow of our lives.

Since making even small changes can be traumatic, a paradigm shift can be experienced as total upheaval. One person described it this way: "I was going along fine, and then someone pressed the fast-forward button." This is especially difficult for people who have developed a vested interest in their current facts, beliefs, values and behaviors. They want to believe their facts are accurate, their beliefs are true, good and effective predictors, their values are the best ones, and their behavior represents the correct choices. It can be devastating, therefore, when they find out that their whole way of thinking and acting needs to be revamped.

Talking about a paradigm shift can be a stimulating intellectual exercise, but actually making one is often gut wrenching—what Morris Massey (1989) calls a *significant emotional event*. When I found myself unemployed shortly after my 50th birthday, I was forced to think about my career from an entirely different perspective, one that I never anticipated. On several occasions I woke up in a cold sweat, wondering if I could cope with the ambiguity of my situation. To keep from being overwhelmed by anxiety, I remembered what I told my clients: focus on what you can learn instead of your emotions, because learning empowers you to move forward. During that period I learned that uncertainty had become a permanent part of my life, so I had to find ways to thrive in spite of it. I also learned that instead of reinventing my career once, I would have to do it over and over again.

Whether your goal is to keep pace with the new organizational reality yourself or to help other people do this, I've found that the following questions greatly facilitate this process:

What Is Your Need?

During times of uncertainty or confusion, anxiety often leads people to rush to solutions before being clear about what they want to accomplish. As they talk to me about their struggles, therefore, I find it helpful to ask such questions as, "What is your need?", "What is your purpose?", "What are your objectives?", or "What are you trying to accomplish?" This offers them a starting point, so they can think about the issues more rationally and begin developing a systematic plan of action. It also allows them to feel less overwhelmed and more in control of their experience. While in the midst of my own personal paradigm shift, I reminded myself that what I needed most was a fresh outlook on my career, not just a job. Thus I was able to focus on the forest, not just the trees.

What Are Your Facts? Are Your Facts Accurate And Complete?

A paradigm shift begins with significant changes in facts or objective reality. A good example is what has happened in the world of work during the past 200 years. First we had the Agricultural Revolution, and then came the Industrial Revolution, and now we're in the Information Age. Table 4.1 offers a summary of the number of Americans in different occupations as we've moved into the Information Age.

Table 4.1

U.S. Occupational Shifts during the 20th Century

Declining Occupations:	Present	Past	
Railroad workers	231,000	2,076,000	1920
Carriage and harness makers	*	109,000	1900
Telegraph operators	8,000	75,000	1920
Boilermakers	*	74,000	1920
Milliners	*	100,000	1910
Cobblers	25,000	102,000	1900
Blacksmiths	*	238,000	1910
Watchmakers	*	101,000	1920
Switchboard operators	213,000	421,000	1970
Farm workers	813,000	11,533,000	1910

Rising Occupations:			
Airline pilots and mechanics	232,000	0	1900
Medical technicians	1,379,000	0	1910
Engineers	1,846,000	38,000	1900
Computer programmers/operators	1,287,000	*	1960
Fax machine operators	699,000	0	1980
Auto mechanics	864,000	0	1900
Truck, bus and taxi drivers	3,328,000	0	1900
Professional athletes	77,000	*	1920
TV and radio announcers	60,000	*	1930
Electricians/electronic repairers	711,000	51,000	1900
Optometrists	62,000	*	1910

* Less than 5,000
Source: U.S. Bureau of the Census

In his book, *The End of Affluence*, Jeffrey Madrick (1995) indicates that during the late 1800s, the service economy accounted for 33% of our gross national product. That figure grew to 66% after World War II, to 75% by the late 1970s, and to over 80% today. By carefully examining the list of declining and rising occupations in Table 4.1, it's easy to see that most of the increases are in the service sector. These changes have brought about a tremendous upheaval in the job market. Thousands upon thousands of adults who thought they were set for life are returning to school for retraining, because their current abilities (knowledge and skills) are no longer in demand.

Another major trend is the increasing competitiveness of other countries. While the United States essentially controlled the world market until the late 1950s, that's no longer the case. Many other countries can now meet or exceed the U.S. in terms of productivity, cost and quality. For example, in the 1960s East Asia accounted for only 4% of the world's economic output, but it accounts for more than 25% now. Also, in 1950, the U.S. produced 76% of all motor vehicles, but it only produced 25% in 1994. In an effort to remain competitive, U.S. firms have had to make major changes in quality and efficiency.

When preparing for change, whether personal or organizational, the first step is to gather up-to-date information that is accurate, complete and free from distortion. Inaccurate, incomplete or distorted information is not only useless, but it can be harmful.

What Are Your Beliefs? Are Your Beliefs Empirically-Based? What Evidence Do You Have?

Beliefs are subjective assumptions, opinions, conclusions, and predictions. Beliefs are more important than facts, because they represent the meaning people attach to factual information. By themselves facts don't serve as motives, but the meanings people attach to facts can be powerful motives. Since beliefs are subjective variables and not objective realities, their usefulness doesn't depend on whether they're popular but on whether they're *viable* (workable, helpful, and useful). Beliefs should be evaluated by their results, not by how good or bad they may sound. Viable beliefs will be accurately grounded on facts, making them empirically-based, while nonviable beliefs will lack empirical evidence. In evaluating the viability of specific beliefs, some useful questions to ask are:

- "What proof do you have?"

- "What other factors should we consider?"

- "Could these facts be explained in any other way?"

- "Should we gather more information before going with this conclusion?"

- "Do your beliefs allow you to meet your needs? If not, then what good are they? Why fight to keep them?"

Tables 4.2, 4.3, and 4.4 provide some examples of viable and unviable beliefs about self, others and the organization in the present economic climate. Notice that in almost every instance the viable and unviable beliefs are exactly the opposite. Viable beliefs now emphasize taking responsibility for oneself, facing reality directly, diversifying one's knowledge, skills and experience, seeking opportunities in the midst of uncertainty, building relationships based on trust, cooperation and mutual respect, placing the needs of the customer first, taking risks rather than taking orders, and being a leader instead of a follower. Security no longer resides in what others can give us, but in what we can do.

Radical differences exist between the viable and unviable beliefs highlighted in these tables. Many people have and will continue to fall by the wayside because, in spite of their best effort, they aren't capable of making the necessary changes, while many others don't want to make such changes and resist them. I served as a consultant for one organization where managers decided whether or not to keep people based on their beliefs about who could and couldn't embrace the team concept. During another consulting assignment, a key manager quit because he didn't want to share control with a team. In my opinion, among the total work force only a small percentage will come to embrace the current, viable beliefs, and find creative ways to thrive within the present conditions. One of the primary purposes of this book is to help increase that percentage. It's important to remember, however, that while certain beliefs may be viable now, they may not be viable in the future (many of the unviable beliefs listed below were once viable). The key thing is to continually seek out new information, and then update your beliefs to reflect that information.

Table 4.2

Viable/Unviable Beliefs about Yourself

UNVIABLE	VIABLE
I wouldn't be able to survive if I lost my job.	If I lost my job, I could use my knowledge and skills elsewhere.
I can take the safe way.	There is no safe way.
The change won't impact me.	The change will impact everyone.
I've worked hard to get where I am, I deserve it.	If I try to rest on yesterday's laurels I'll fall behind.
The organization is responsible for my security.	I'm responsible for my own security.
Once I'm secure I can be creative.	Security is the enemy of creativity.
It's dangerous to take risks.	It's dangerous to keep doing things the old way.
I know my job well enough already, I don't need to grow.	Grow or die.
I can hang on until I retire.	If I just try to hang on, I'll stifle myself and the organization.
I better not admit to mistakes, it might get me in trouble.	I must take responsibility for mistakes and try to learn from them.
All I need to know is my own job.	I need to know about a lot of jobs.

Table 4.3

Viable/Unviable Beliefs about Other People

UNVIABLE	VIABLE
I don't need other people, I can depend on myself.	We need to depend on each other to beat the competition.
Individuals are usually more creative than teams.	Teams are usually more creative than individuals.
The best ideas come from management.	Good ideas can come from anywhere in the organization.
Don't trust co-workers, they might be after your job.	You have to trust co-workers to focus on the competition.
You need power and control to get people to do their work.	Power and control inhibit creativity and cause resentment.
Sharing information gives others power over you.	Sharing information is necessary to achieve mutual goals.
You have to protect your own turf.	While you're protecting your turf, the competition is gaining on you.
Managers should be bosses.	Managers should be coaches.

Table 4.4
Viable/Unviable Beliefs about the Organization

UNVIABLE	VIABLE
We can remain the same and survive.	We need to change to survive.
Things will remain the same or change slowly.	Things will never be the same and change will be rapid.
The organization will always be here.	The organization must remain competitive to survive.
Security is in the organization.	Security is in your knowledge, skills and experience.
People with seniority will be protected.	People need to add value, not just put in time.
Conformity is the key to success.	Versatility is the key to success.
The organization owes me for my service.	The organization pays me for my service.
The organization will look out for my interests.	The organization will look out for its own interests.
We work for the organization.	We work for the customer; the organization is where the work is done.
I've done my job, if the customer doesn't like it that's their problem.	My job isn't complete until the customer is satisfied.
Communication works best top-down.	Any barrier to communication is harmful.
Our products/services are already good enough.	Our products/services can be offered faster, cheaper and better by someone else.

What Are Your Feelings? What Impact Do Your Feelings Have On Your Decisions?

Feelings are emotional reactions triggered by beliefs (i.e. assumptions, conclusions, and predictions). Generally speaking, empirically-based, rational beliefs tend to produce positive feelings, while non-empirically-based, irrational beliefs tend to produce negative feelings. There are exceptions of course, as when people are confronted with "bad news," but working through the issues posed often restores a person's sense of well-being. Whenever people experience negative feelings, therefore, they should go back and review their facts and the beliefs (i.e. their perception of the facts), ridding themselves of the ones that don't stand up under scrutiny. At the same time, I want to point out that anxiety, while usually considered a negative feeling, isn't always bad. A certain amount of anxiety can be a positive source of motivation. While anxiety stemming from mistaken, inaccurate or distorted facts and beliefs is almost always harmful, it's unrealistic to expect people to make the kind of changes discussed above without being anxious, because they will be acutely aware of their vulnerability.

It's important to remember that desire to succeed and fear of failure go hand in hand. If you didn't care about being successful, then you wouldn't worry about failure. Accordingly, I don't view self-confidence as the absence of anxiety, but rather action in the face of anxiety. Self-confidence is facing reality as it is, even though some aspects of it might be troublesome. People can either try something new in spite of their anxiety, or avoid it because of anxiety. Unfortunately, the world will not wait for those in the latter category to catch up, and will simply leave them behind. When I was going through my own personal paradigm shift I experienced a great deal of anxiety, but I knew I still had to move forward. Doing this increased my self-confidence, but the anxiety never went away completely and remains to this day.

What Are Your Values? Are Your Values Viable?

Values are standards of importance, and serve as the criteria for making decisions and setting priorities. People develop a vested interest in the particular values they embrace. People want to believe that their values are the best ones or even the only ones. Since values are subjective variables, however, they can't be proven right or wrong. One of the biggest misconceptions that people have about values is that they are entirely benevolent and positive aspects of personality. Unfortunately, values can lead to very destructive and negative results. The highest achievements of human beings have been motivated by values, but so have wars, discrimination, hate, crime, riots, and other malevolent human behavior. As with beliefs, therefore, values should be evaluated by their viability, not on how noble or lofty they may sound.

Some values will be more useful than others in the current economic climate. Table 4.5 provides a list of viable and unviable work values. Although many of the values in the unviable column were viable in the past, they have been replaced by values representing their opposites. Gone are the days when lone rangers stacked on top of each other in elaborate hierarchies demand loyalty, control information and bark out commands in order to achieve goals. Today's organizations are flatter and leaner, allowing for greater speed, flexibility and responsiveness. Also gone are the consumers who bought something and felt grateful if it worked. Now consumers are empowered; they demand quality for a reasonable price and take their business elsewhere if they don't get it. Consequently, values for quality, trust, accountability, team performance, networking, risk-taking, empowerment, process improvement and leadership have become imperative for survival.

Again, many people have had and will continue to have trouble making changes of this magnitude. The adjustments required will take them way out of their comfort zone. Nevertheless, perseverance, determination, a willingness to ask for help and to obtain additional training will augur well for eventual success.

Table 4.5
Viable and Unviable Work Values

UNVIABLE	VIABLE
Productivity	Quality
Security	Risk-taking/courage
Tenure/seniority	Adding value
Conformity	Innovativeness
Predictability	Flexibility
Control	Empowerment

UNVIABLE	VIABLE
Independence/dependence	Interdependence
Individual contribution	Team contribution
Internal competition	Cooperation
Personal success	Customer success
Outcome focus	Process focus
Reactive	Proactive
Expediency	Integrity
Formality	Informality
Following procedures	Responsiveness
Privilege/special interests	Inclusiveness
Clear boundaries	Boundaryless
Similarity	Diversity
Traditional education	Life-long learning
Management	Leadership
Tactical	Strategic
Meeting standards	Continuous improvement

Empirically-based, rational beliefs and the positive feelings they produce foster values which enable people to pursue meaningful goals, while non empirically-based, irrational beliefs and the negative feelings they produce foster values designed to protect people from perceived danger. Values in the former category tend to be proactive and empowering, while those in the latter category tend to be reactive and defensive. Even the casual observer of organizational behavior will be aware of the constant ebb and flow between people's desire to accomplish something and their need to protect themselves.

As a counselor, consultant and trainer, one of my objectives is to help people increase the amount of time they spend trying to make good things happen, and decrease the amount of time they spend trying to prevent bad things from happening. The starting point is challenging them to identify any inaccurate facts and unviable beliefs which give rise to fear, and to exchange them for accurate facts and viable, confidence-producing beliefs. At the same time, I encourage them to embrace proactive values that will help them achieve their goals.

As discussed in Chapter 1, our deepest psychological need is to view ourselves and be viewed by others as having worth as a person, and that we endeavor to accomplish this by striving to meet four sub-needs: mastery, a sense of meaning and purpose, respect, and acceptance. In my opinion, there are eight values that are especially viable ways to pursue these sub-needs in the current business climate, two pertaining to each need. Because of their power to serve as a catalyst for success, I refer to them as "megavalues." The relationship between the four sub-needs and eight mega-values is shown in Figure 4.1.

Figure 4.1
Relationship between Needs and Values

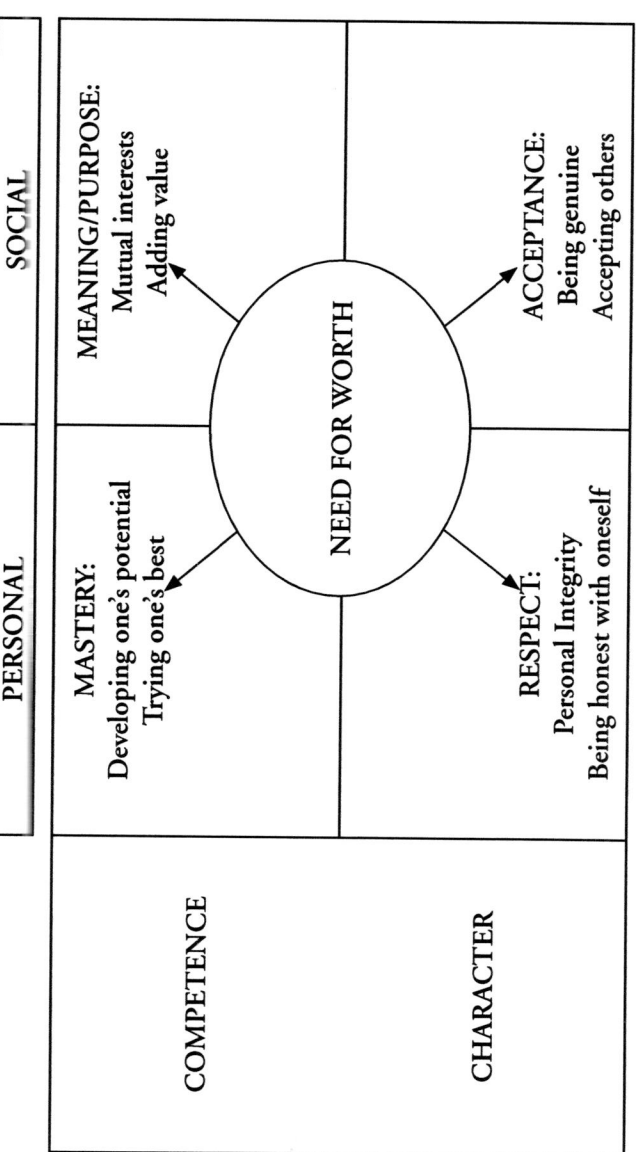

I will now describe the eight mega-values, contrasting them with their opposites, which are the values people often resort to when they find themselves stuck in a reactive, defensive mode.

Developing One's Potential vs. Preserving the Status Quo. Some of the most gut-wrenching consulting I've done has been with large organizations in the midst of downsizing their middle manager ranks. Both the managers let go and the ones remaining face major challenges. Those in the former category feel hurt, angry and betrayed, since many of them believed acceptable performance guaranteed them a job for life. They're also faced with considerable anxiety and uncertainty about their future. Those in the latter category feel angry that their colleagues and friends were severed, guilty yet relieved that they still have a job, and worried about how long that job will last.

The managers in both groups who make the best adjustment are the ones who place a value on developing their potential, as opposed to preserving the status quo. Among those let go, many who cling to the past simply disappear from the work force, unable to cope with the thought of looking for a new job or going back to school, while those believing they still have potential either seek opportunities in the same field or begin retraining for another one. In retrospect, some choosing to develop themselves are actually grateful for having been laid off, because it forced them to make choices that resulted in career enhancement.

Managers surviving a downsizing realize that preserving the status quo is the kiss of death; they'll be required to expand their knowledge and skills if they plan to have a future with the organization. Many of them develop greater self-confidence and eventually become more effective contributors, as they take the initiative to participate in educational programs.

The world of work will continue to experience rapid and unpredictable change. While people won't have very much control over the nature of that change, and job security is a thing of the past, they do have control over developing their potential. By placing an emphasis on learning and growth, they'll increase their chances of remaining viable, whether it's with their current organization or some other endeavor. This is one of the best ways people can empower themselves, fulfilling their need for mastery.

Trying One's Best vs. Trying to Be Perfect. Perfectionism is one the ten inner obstacles Bernstein and Rozen (1994) describe in their book, *Sacred Bull*. People who strive for perfection worry about whether they've done enough or made a mistake, putting pressure on both themselves and all those around them. Compulsively seeking improvement perfectionists tend to micro-manage people, sending the message that they lack confidence in what others can do. They fill the work environment with pressure and tension, as others feel that their work is constantly under scrutiny.

Trying to be perfect isn't viable because people don't have control over all the factors affecting performance. No matter how hard people strive to dot every *i* and cross every *t*, something always seems to happen to upset best laid plans. In contrast, trying one's best is within people's control and, therefore, much more viable. Whereas fear of making mistakes keeps perfectionists from being able to enjoy their work, those trying their best can relax and find pleasure in using their talents and abilities. Even if something doesn't work out, they have consolation in knowing they did all they could, rather than wondering if they could or should have done more. This frame of mind also allows them to be a source of support and encouragement to others in the workplace.

Concern for Mutual Interests vs. Concern for Self-Interest. Peter Block (1996) talks about the importance of focusing on mutual interests in his book, *Stewardship: Choosing service over self-interest*. And Stephen Covey (1989) identifies "Think Win Win" as one of the seven habits of highly effective people, by which he means caring that other people win as well as yourself. In my experience people can be divided into two camps: those who show concern for others, and those who are just concerned for themselves. Upon the former, co-workers heap accolades, saying such things as, "He's a team player," "Whenever I ask her for help, she always goes the extra mile," or "He puts the interests of others above his own." Upon the latter, co-workers heap disdain, saying such things as, "The only one she cares about is herself," "He'll only help you if there's something in it for him," or "Never turn your back on him; he'll walk all over you to get ahead." Obviously, people are much more likely to trust those concerned about mutual interests than those concerned about self-interest. Although we don't have control over whether people look out for our interests, we can still choose to look out for their interests.

A team never becomes cohesive if members perceive each other as only looking out for themselves, or if they believe they can accomplish their goals without each other. It's only when team members show genuine concern for each other and have a sense of interdependence that they're able to flourish. Working with others toward common goals helps people meet their need for a sense of meaning and purpose. People tend to focus on self-interest when they don't trust others to take their needs into consideration. Making it clear that people are expected to work together toward mutual interests can help them build a greater level of trust.

Adding Value vs. Seeking Recognition. People seeking recognition try to draw attention to their work and take credit for success, while people seeking to add value focus on making a contribution and sharing success. Co-workers avoid those who toot their own horn, but gravitate toward those willing to be team players.

One of the best ways to add value in an organization is by listening. "Seek first to understand, then to be understood," is another one of Stephen Covey's seven habits. When I was going through my own personal paradigm shift, I took an inventory of my professional skills. While serving as a facilitator, the ability to synthesize data and diagnose problems were high on the list, I concluded that listening to people and trying to convey that I understood what they were saying were my most important skills. I think people have sought me out over the years as a counselor and consultant primarily because they sensed that I would listen.

People have a deep need to be understood; I have this need myself. Feeling understood allows people to feel less isolated and instills in them a sense of hope when they're discouraged. People have often made comments to me like, "Thanks for listening," "I don't feel so alone anymore," "I feel so much better now," or "I've gained a fresh perspective on my situation, just because you let me talk about it." This, in turn, has allowed me to feel that I've contributed something to other people, helping me to meet my need for a sense of meaning and purpose. While people don't have control over whether others listen to them, they do have control over listening to others.

Unfortunately, people seldom trust others to listen. It's commonplace to hear remarks like, "No one listens to me," "No one understands me," or "No one cares what I think." When people feel this way, they tend to either remain silent or talk more in an effort to be understood. I've facilitated team meetings where everyone was clamoring for attention and no one was listening. Voices would increase in volume as people competed for air time. When this happens, I like to call a time out and ask, "Does anyone here feel understood?" This rhetorical question forces team members to step back and examine their pattern of interaction, and to establish norms requiring people to listen and convey understanding before expressing their own views. When people begin trusting others to listen, this frees them up to listen in return.

Personal Integrity vs. Expediency. The subject of integrity has been the focus of increasing interest in the professional literature, as evidenced by the publication of books like, *The power of ethical management*, by Ken Blanchard and Norman Vincent Peale (1988), and *Leadership and the quest for integrity*, by Joseph Badaracco, Jr. and Richard Ellsworth (1989). People want to view themselves and to be viewed by others as being moral and ethical. An unwritten code of ethics exists between people. As they deal with each other, they have a sense for what's right and wrong. We refer to this as "common sense." While people don't always have control over the circumstances, they can still decide to do what they believe is right. People who act out of integrity inspire confidence and trust, which helps them meet their need for respect. People who act out of expediency, however, inspire suspicion and doubt. Beyond that, they often rationalize their actions in order to maintain their self-esteem, creating even more suspicion.

While some people are unscrupulous and try to take advantage of others, in my experience most people choose expediency over integrity in response to some perceived danger, real or imagined. Helping them identify and deal with the danger can create the conditions necessary for them to restore their integrity. This will not only allow them to feel better about themselves, but will allow other people to feel better about them.

Being Honest with Oneself vs. Self-Justification. Some people have a strong enough sense of self-worth to be honest with themselves about their strengths and weaknesses, while others attempt to maintain self-worth by avoiding anything that might reflect on them negatively. Those in the former category take responsibility for their actions, regarding corrective feedback as an opportunity to increase their effectiveness. As such, this type of honesty serves the purpose of helping people develop their potential. Those in the latter category, however, externalize responsibility for their actions. Corrective feedback is viewed as threatening, so they tend to respond to it defensively. When confronted with a problem, therefore, they deny, rationalize, minimize, or blame others. Since they don't learn from their mistakes, they're doomed to repeat them.

In addition to fostering personal and career growth, being honest with oneself allows people to serve as good role models for others seeking to learn effective organizational behaviors. When those in leadership positions take responsibility for their mistakes and seek corrective feedback from others, including subordinates, it removes fear from relationships, and revolutionizes the performance appraisal process. This is one of the best ways to act on W. Edwards Deming's management principle, *drive out fear*. While being honest with oneself takes courage, it provides others with an example worthy of emulation.

Being Genuine vs. Posturing. It is one of people's deepest desires to be authentic or real with others, and to have others be real with them. This helps them meet their need for acceptance. While people crave this kind of openness, fear of being rejected, humiliated or embarrassed make it a rarity in organizational life. In fact, after having worked with thousands of people in many organizations for over 30 years, I estimate that about 80% of the interaction between people represents posturing—the dynamics are tainted by "hidden agendas"—while only about 20% are genuine. How many times have you sat through a meeting where two people were having a very diplomatic exchange, only to have someone tell you later what he/she *really* thinks. Even during these moments of candor, however, it's difficult to tell if the person is being honest with you or has a hidden agenda. This sort of drama takes place every day in every organization.

People are often skeptical that others are being genuine with them, so they play their cards close to the vest, only being genuine after determining that it's "safe." Since it's difficult to tell if it really is safe, however, people tend to err on the side of posturing. They wait to see if others are authentic before being authentic themselves, but this means everyone wastes a lot of time waiting. It takes courage to let your guard down when you are unsure how others will respond, but this is more viable than spending eight hours a day pretending to be someone you aren't. Another good reason for doing this is that genuineness is infectious; if you take the initiative to be yourself, it frees others up to be themselves. This helps to create a healthier interpersonal environment in the workplace.

Accepting Others vs. Judging Others. People want to believe that they're okay as they are now, not that they have to change in order to be okay. This helps them meet their need for acceptance, which is essential for the development of a cohesive team. Whenever people enter a new job situation they're asking themselves such questions as, "What are the ground rules here?", "How are people expected to act?", "What goes and what doesn't?" During their first several months of employment—the honeymoon period—most people make an effort to fit in, but they're also looking for a way to express their individuality and uniqueness. The tension between conformity and individuality can have a powerful effect on employee morale. Over the years, I've heard many people say such things as, "They expect us to act like robots," "I can't be myself around here," "I've got to get out of this place, it's too stifling for me."

When people feel insecure they tend to act the way they think others want them to act, keeping their individuality hidden. What they say and do becomes very stilted, as they continually try to please others. The problem with this is that we can't control the acceptance others offer us; we can only control the acceptance we offer them. The best way to receive acceptance is to give it.

A related issue is prejudice in the workplace. People want to be judged by their work performance, not by external characteristics, such as race, gender, age, ethnicity, religion, lifestyle or socio-economic class. Showing respect for differences allows people to feel like they belong. In contrast, discrimination creates a hostile work environment. People tend to be judgmental when they lack understanding of differences or feel threatened by them.

Unfortunately, it's unrealistic to expect that we can eradicate prejudice, since people's attitudes toward differences are often deeply ingrained. We can, however, make it clear that there's no place for discrimination in the organization. Also, we can encourage training programs designed to increase understanding of differences, and behave in ways that demonstrate a commitment to fostering diversity and inclusiveness.

A summary of the eight mega-values, emphasizing the areas over which you have control, is provided in Table 4.6.

Table 4.6
Pursuing Viable Values Gives You Control

MEGA-VALUE CHOICES	YOUR AREA OF CONTROL
Developing One's Potential vs. Preserving the Status Quo	You have control over whether or not you seek out learning opportunities.
Trying One's Best vs. Trying to Be Perfect	You have control over using your talents and abilities to the fullest.
Concern for Mutual Interest vs. Concern for Self-Interest	You have control over whether or not you're willing to give to others.

MEGA-VALUE CHOICES	YOUR AREA OF CONTROL
Adding Value vs. Seeking Recognition	You have control over contributing to the common good.
Personal Integrity vs. Expediency	You have control over showing others you can be trusted.
Being Honest With Oneself vs. Seeking to Justify Oneself	You have control over whether or not you're honest with yourself.
Being Genuine vs. Posturing	You have control over whether or not you're honest with others.
Accepting Others vs. Judging Others	You have control over whether you accept people for who they are.

What Are Your Behaviors? Are Your Behaviors Effective?

While accurate facts, viable beliefs and values are prerequisites to effective behaviors, they aren't sufficient, because many behaviors require a high level of knowledge and skill. If people lack the necessary knowledge and skills, therefore, they must be willing to obtain additional education and training. This is crucial because the work world doesn't evaluate people on their beliefs and values, but on their actions. Table 4.7 offers a summary of the behaviors required for people to be effective in today's organizations. As you can see, these behaviors are consistent with the viable beliefs and values discussed above.

Table 4.7
Effective and Ineffective Behaviors

INEFFECTIVE	EFFECTIVE
Staying with the familiar	Exploring new possibilities
Deferring to authority	Assertiveness
Talking	Listening
Pointing the finger, passing the blame.	Taking responsibility for one's actions.
Manipulating	Dealing with issues directly
Withholding information	Sharing information
Protecting turf	Networking

INEFFECTIVE	EFFECTIVE
Gaining and keeping power	Sharing power
Doing the minimum to get by	Doing whatever it takes
Discriminating against others	Respecting differences
Focusing on self-interests	Focusing on mutual interests
Holding others back	Encouraging others
Following orders	Taking the initiative
Seeking win-lose outcomes	Seeking win-win outcomes

Is Your Need Met? If Not, How Can You Meet The Need?

The bottom line for everything discussed in this chapter can be summarized by this question: Did you meet your need or didn't you? If so, you can go on to your next need. If not, it's important to reexamine your facts, beliefs, values and behaviors, and be prepared to make the changes required to meet your need. Having the courage to confront and change your thoughts, feelings, decisions and behaviors will increase your chances of being successful, and it will give you the credibility required to lead others through change. The Megavalue Scale™ and Plan for Personal Change allow you to assess the degree to which your decisions are motivated by values that are viable in the current business climate.

MEGAVALUE SCALE™
AND PLAN FOR PERSONAL CHANGE

PURPOSE: To assess the degree to which your values, beliefs, and behaviors are viable in the current business climate, and set goals for increasing the effectiveness of your values, beliefs, and behaviors. The Megavalue Scale™ (40 items) takes 30 minutes to complete, while the Plan for Personal Change takes one hour.

Procedures for the Megavalue Scale™

- EXPLAIN that participants will now have an opportunity to assess their current values.

- HAND OUT a copy of the Megavalue Scale™ to each participant, including the instrument itself, scoring instruction sheet and Megavalue Profile.

- GIVE instructions for completing the instrument, calculating scores, and plotting the Profile:

  First read each of the 40 items and circle the response that best applies to you. These are hard questions to answer, requiring you to face yourself honestly.

  Then calculate your scores for each value continuum.

  Once you've totaled all your scores, you have your Megavalue Profile.

  You will not be asked to share this information with anyone. This is strictly for your own learning.

- After everyone has completed their Megavalue Profile, EXPLAIN how to interpret the results:

  The higher your scores, the more viable your values will be in the current business climate.

  Low scores reveal areas where improvement is needed.

- ASK for comments and reactions.

Procedures for the Plan for Personal Change

- EXPLAIN the purpose for the Plan for Personal Change:

  You will now have a chance to pull together what you've learned about viable/unviable beliefs and values, effective/ineffective behaviors, and your current values, and decide what changes you want to make to foster your personal growth.

- HAND OUT the two-page Plan for Personal Change, and GIVE instructions for completing it:

  Individually, identify values you'd like to emphasize more fully, unviable beliefs you'd like to change, more viable beliefs you can substitute for the unviable ones, and new behaviors you plan to try out, in support of your viable beliefs and values.

  Take about 15 minutes to do this.

- DIVIDE participants into subgroups of 4-6 and GIVE the following instructions:

  Now take turns sharing your plan with the others in your subgroup, seeking their feedback and suggestions.

  You will have 45 minutes for this discussion.

- DEBRIEF key learning points with the whole group:

  What did you get out of this exercise?

  How did your teammates help you make decisions about what to do differently?

  What were the most helpful suggestions you received?

  Any aha's?

The Megavalue Scale™

by
Ken Hultman

Instructions

The Megavalue Scale™ is designed to assess the degree to which your decisions are motivated by values that are viable in the current business climate.

First, read each item and circle the response that best applies to you. Next, calculate your scores, and then complete the Megavalue Profile. These are tough questions requiring careful thought and reflection. As you answer them, please be honest with yourself; otherwise the results will be meaningless. This is feedback for you only. You won't be required to share the information with anyone else.

In my daily work I:

		Almost Never				Almost Always
1.	avoid trying new things	4	3	2	1	0
2.	strive to be perfect	4	3	2	1	0
3.	keep information to myself	4	3	2	1	0
4.	draw attention to my work	4	3	2	1	0
5.	compromise what I believe is right to stay out of trouble	4	3	2	1	0
6.	avoid thinking about things that make me feel bad about myself	4	3	2	1	0
7.	pretend to agree with others	4	3	2	1	0
8.	evaluate people on the basis of external characteristics	4	3	2	1	0
9.	prefer using my current skills to developing new ones	4	3	2	1	0
10.	get frustrated if I can't do something right	4	3	2	1	0
11.	focus on getting what I want	4	3	2	1	0
12.	try to impress others	4	3	2	1	0
13.	bend the truth, if necessary to protect myself	4	3	2	1	0
14.	make excuses for myself	4	3	2	1	0
15.	talk about people behind their back	4	3	2	1	0
16.	feel uneasy around people different from me	4	3	2	1	0
17.	fail to take advantage of learning opportunities	4	3	2	1	0
18.	put myself down when I make a mistake	4	3	2	1	0
19.	share information when it's to my advantage	4	3	2	1	0
20.	try to compete with co-workers	4	3	2	1	0
21.	let the end justify the means	4	3	2	1	0
22.	blame others or circumstances when something goes wrong	4	3	2	1	0
23.	tell people what I think they want to hear	4	3	2	1	0
24.	avoid people who are different from me	4	3	2	1	0
25.	resist change	4	3	2	1	0
26.	focus on what I do wrong rather than what I do right	4	3	2	1	0
27.	look out for my own interests	4	3	2	1	0
28.	seek recognition for my work	4	3	2	1	0
29.	cut corners to get the job done	4	3	2	1	0
30.	minimize my mistakes	4	3	2	1	0
31.	keep my real thoughts and feelings to myself	4	3	2	1	0

In my daily work I:

		Almost Never			Almost Always	
32.	regard people different from me less favorably	4	3	2	1	0
33.	try to get by on what I know already	4	3	2	1	0
34.	blow small mistakes out of proportion	4	3	2	1	0
35.	offer help when I have something to gain	4	3	2	1	0
36.	prefer giving my views instead of listening to the views of others	4	3	2	1	0
37.	look for ways to get around the rules	4	3	2	1	0
38.	deny my shortcomings	4	3	2	1	0
39.	choose what I say very carefully	4	3	2	1	0
40.	prefer to be around people holding similar views	4	3	2	1	0

Calculating Your Scores

This instrument consists of eight value choices with five items for each. To develop your own Megavalue Profile:

1. On the worksheet below, total the scores you gave yourself for the five items pertaining to each value choice.

2. Place a dot at the corresponding point for each value on the Megavalue Profile.

3. Connect the dots with a line.

DEVELOPING ONE'S POTENTIAL	TRYING ONE'S BEST	CONCERN FOR MUTUAL INTERESTS	ADDING VALUE
1 ____	2 ____	3 ____	4 ____
9 ____	10 ____	11 ____	12 ____
17 ____	18 ____	19 ____	20 ____
25 ____	26 ____	27 ____	28 ____
33 ____	34 ____	35 ____	36 ____
TOTAL ____	TOTAL ____	TOTAL ____	TOTAL ____

PERSONAL INTEGRITY	BEING HONEST WITH ONESELF	BEING GENUINE	ACCEPTING OTHERS
5 ____	6 ____	7 ____	8 ____
13 ____	14 ____	15 ____	16 ____
21 ____	22 ____	23 ____	24 ____
29 ____	30 ____	31 ____	32 ____
37 ____	38 ____	39 ____	40 ____
TOTAL ____	TOTAL ____	TOTAL ____	TOTAL ____

Megavalue Profile

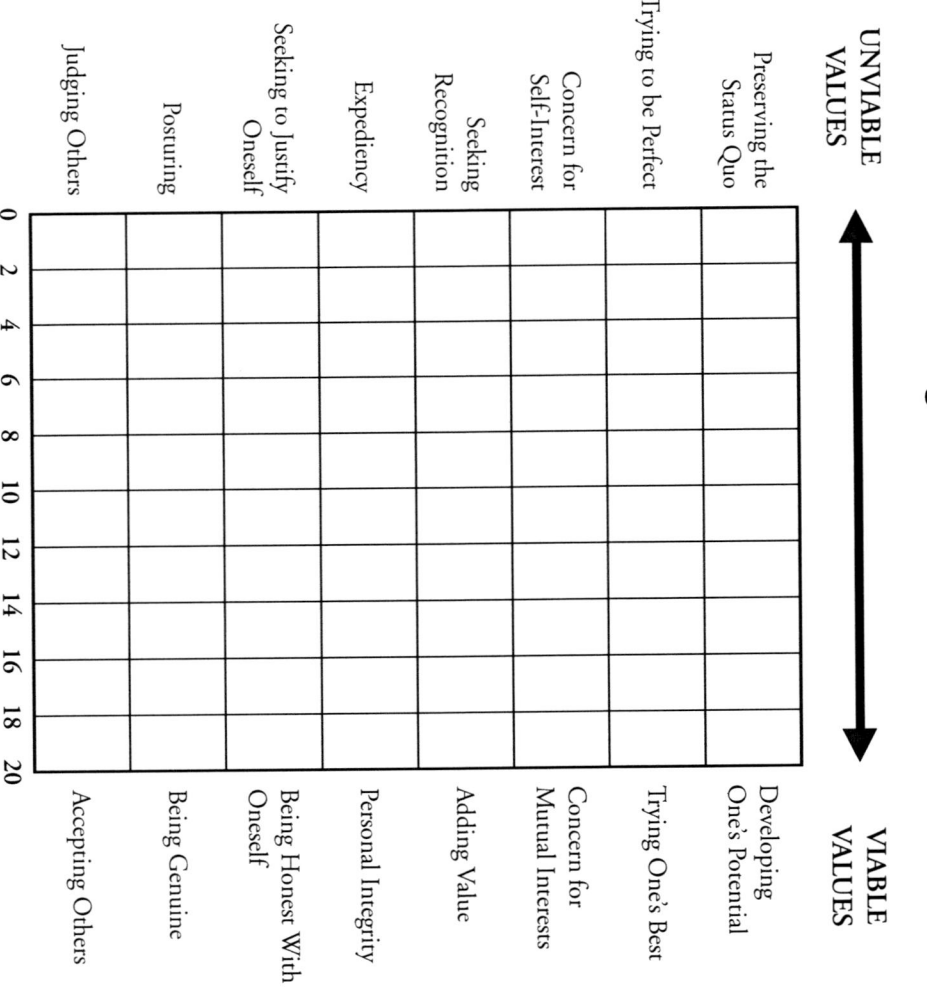

UNVIABLE VALUES		VIABLE VALUES

Preserving the Status Quo — Developing One's Potential

Trying to be Perfect — Trying One's Best

Concern for Self-Interest — Concern for Mutual Interests

Seeking Recognition — Adding Value

Expediency — Personal Integrity

Seeking to Justify Oneself — Being Honest With Oneself

Posturing — Being Genuine

Judging Others — Accepting Others

Scale: 0 2 4 6 8 10 12 14 16 18 20

By examining the Profile, you can see which of your values are more viable than others. High scores reveal areas of strength, while low scores reveal areas where improvement is needed.

Plan for Personal Change

On the next two pages develop a personal plan that will allow you to implement more viable values and beliefs, and more effective behaviors.

1 Identify values you'd like to emphasize more fully.	2 Identify unviable beliefs you'd like to change.	3 Identify more viable beliefs you can substitute for the unviable ones.

Identify new behaviors you plan to try out, in support of your viable beliefs and values.

4

PART 3

VALUES-DRIVEN ORGANIZATIONAL CHANGE

5. Identifying and Overcoming Resistance to Change

Presents a conceptual framework for understanding resistance to organizational change, and includes the Change Opinion Survey™, which can be used to assess resistance. Also includes several exercises for assessing resistance and planning change.

6. Building an Adaptive Organization

Presents the Adaptive Organization Scale, which can be used to assess an organization's current and desired operating practices, and determine how it can become more adaptive to changing conditions.

5

IDENTIFYING AND OVERCOMING RESISTANCE TO CHANGE

PURPOSE: To present a conceptual framework for understanding resistance to organizational change, along with guidelines and tools for assessing and dealing with it.

The toughest challenge of organizational leaders today is to manage at the speed of change. With the breathtaking pace of technological advancement that will only continue to escalate, and the doubling of knowledge every 5 years, leaders face tremendous pressure as they try to gain support for change. Research on corporate culture by Kotter and Heskett (1992) has shown that organizations will not be able to sustain excellent performance over the long haul unless they have values and norms allowing them to adapt to a changing environment. Regardless of how good or necessary a change may be, resistance should be expected. A survey of 500 executives conducted by William Schiemann (1992) concluded that resistance was the main reason why organizational changes fail. A study by Hammer and Associates found that 60% of the reengineering projects that failed were due to employee resistance (Moomough, 1999). While preventing resistance completely is an unrealistic goal, the ability to manage resistance effectively has emerged as an essential skill. This article will help you do that by offering a conceptual framework for understanding resistance, and also practical suggestions for assessing and overcoming it.

Understanding Resistance

When people talk about resistance, they usually refer to specific behaviors observed in others. Thus it's commonplace to hear someone say, "He's resisting these new procedures," or "She's refusing to go along with the changes." Behaviors used to resist change fall into two categories: *active* and *passive* resistance. Some examples of both types are included in Table 5.1. Behaviors such as these tell us that people are resisting change; however, they don't tell us *why*. The reason for this is that behaviors are external manifestations of internal issues within a person's mindset. In other words, behaviors are symptoms while mindset issues are causes. These distinctions lead to a definition of resistance. *Resistance* is a state of mind reflecting unwillingness or un-receptiveness to change in the ways we think and behave. Resistance can be contrasted with readiness, which is a state of mind reflecting willingness or receptiveness to change. Resistance manifests itself behaviorally by either active opposition to change or by attempting to escape or avoid it; readiness is manifested behaviorally by either active initiation of change or by cooperation with it.

Readiness is not the opposite of resistance, since an absence of resistance doesn't necessarily mean that someone is receptive to change. Other factors, such as lack of information, lack of knowledge or skill, or an immediate need to attend to other matters, could interfere with readiness. Nevertheless, anything that causes resistance can be expected to undermine readiness at any point in time.

Table 5.1
Active and Passive Resistance

ACTIVE RESISTANCE

Being critical	Blaming/accusing	Blocking
Fault-Finding	Sabotaging	Undermining
Ridiculing	Intimidating/threatening	Starting rumors
Appealing to fear	Manipulating	Arguing
Using facts selectively	Distorting facts	Raising objections

PASSIVE RESISTANCE

Agreeing verbally but not following through.
Failing to implement change.
Procrastinating/dragging feet.
Feigning ignorance
Withholding information, suggestions, help or support.
Standing by and allowing the change to fail.

The most important factors making up a person's state of mind are his or her facts, beliefs and values. Facts are objective realities that can be proven with evidence ("We tried that before"), while beliefs are subjective assumptions, conclusions, and predictions ("It didn't work then; it won't work now"). Values are people's conceptions about what is important in life ("I want to be open and honest with everyone about this").

A clear distinction between beliefs and facts is essential, because people often state beliefs as facts ("I know I'm right, so what's the problem?"). Facts can be proven with empirical evidence, while beliefs are subjective assumptions, conclusions, or predictions. In the thinking process, beliefs are more important than facts because they represent the meaning attached to factual information. We all know that facts are subject to distortion; two people exposed to the same set of facts can arrive at entirely different conclusions. Nevertheless, most adults have beliefs held with such high confidence that they treat them as facts. Beliefs of this kind are less amenable to change because they are regarded as irrefutable. When this happens, people are assuming that their beliefs and reality are identical. In one sense there is some truth to this. People's beliefs are their way of understanding themselves, other people, and the world around them. In essence, their beliefs become reality for them. It is indeed a mistake, however, when people conclude that their beliefs represent the one true concept of reality.

Since beliefs are subjective variables and not objective realities, their usefulness doesn't depend on whether they're popular but on whether they're *viable* (workable, helpful, useful). Beliefs should be evaluated by their results, not by how good or bad they may sound. Viable beliefs will be accurately grounded on facts, making them reality-based, while nonviable beliefs will lack empirical evidence.

Thinking is a cognitive process, guided chiefly by one's facts and beliefs. In contrast, feelings have to do with emotions. Without feelings we might be able to think, but we would respond like robots. There's a strong relationship between the cognitive process of thinking, on the one hand, and feelings on the other. By themselves facts are neutral—they don't evoke any feelings. One person could look at a set of facts and ask, "What's all the fuss about?", while another person bellows, "The sky is falling!" It's the assumptions, conclusions, and predictions derived from facts that trigger feelings. The reason for this is that our mind can't distinguish between a real and an imagined threat. If we interpret an event as a threat, for example, our body releases adrenaline and we experience the emotion of fear, whether or not there's anything to be afraid of. Those feelings, in turn, influence our decisions and behaviors for better or for worse.

In addition to facts and beliefs, values are a crucial part of a person's state of mind. Once established, values become our criteria for making decisions and setting priorities. When evaluating a number of alternatives, we eliminate the ones that don't measure up to our standards. Some common values in organizations today are quality, learning, customer satisfaction, mutual interests, integrity, collaboration, and teamwork. Values are to people what instincts are to animals. Since animals can think and feel in varying degrees, it is the ability to establish values that makes us truly unique. Without this capacity, we couldn't be held accountable for our actions.

People have a vested interest in their values. Everyone wants to believe their values are the best ones or even the only ones. Since values are subjective variables, however, they can't be proven right or wrong. As with beliefs, therefore, values should be evaluated by their viability, not by how noble or lofty they may sound. Rational beliefs and the positive feelings they produce lead to values that foster growth; irrational beliefs and the negative feelings they produce lead to defensive values.

Any belief, value or behavior that has been previously successful in meeting our physical, emotional, psychological, and spiritual needs will resist change. Beliefs, values, and behaviors which have been consistently reinforced through experience will be the most resistant to change. In contrast, beliefs, values and behaviors that are less reliable in meeting needs will be more amenable to change. The degree of personal investment will be greater for the former than the latter. People develop such a strong commitment to their most reliable beliefs, values and behaviors that they have trouble thinking about themselves apart from them. In reality, they and their beliefs, values and behaviors become synonymous.

When people perceive that an established belief, value, or behavior is being threatened they experience fear and assume a defensive posture. The intensity of the fear can vary from mild to extreme, depending upon the degree of perceived threat.

Positive and Negative Resistance

Change can be defined as doing something new or differently. By itself, change is neither inherently good nor bad. Any change will make people different from what they were before. There's no such thing as a change with a neutral impact: people will either be better or worse off because of it. Anyone suggesting change should always be aware of this. Although change can be evaluated by its consequences, it's impossible to know in advance how a change will turn out. After taking all the relevant factors into consideration, there are times when it's prudent not to change.

Similarly, there are other times when resistance has a negative connotation. This is a misconception. Sometimes resistance is the most effective response. If people's beliefs, values and behaviors provide them with constructive ways of meeting needs, then it's adaptive and healthy to hold onto them, and resist change. Some changes could disrupt this process and cause the person to become disorganized and less productive. In these situations it is in a person's best interests to resist change.

Thus, there are times when resistance is a *problem* and times when it's a *solution*. The focus of this article is on resistance that is considered a problem. We will now turn our attention to assessing this type of resistance.

Assessing Resistance

Finding the causes of resistance requires us to understand people's facts, beliefs and values. Since we can't literally *see* a person's facts, beliefs and values, the role they play in creating resistance can be difficult to isolate. Fortunately, we have a powerful source of information to help us with this task: observation of what people do and say. Everything someone does or says provides clues about the role these variables play in resistance. Therefore, when observing what someone does, ask yourself, *"What fact, belief, or value is being reflected by what this person is doing?"* Similarly, when listening to someone, ask yourself, *"What fact, belief, or value is being conveyed by what this person is saying?"* By consistently asking yourself these questions and putting the data together, not only will you come to understand people more fully, but also you will be able to more effectively locate the causes of resistance when it occurs.

It's risky to try to assess the causes of resistance by observing only what a person does. It's easy to misinterpret other's behavior. Watching people in action definitely supplies clues, but additional information from what they say is almost always necessary to achieve an accurate assessment. While it's possible for resistance to stem from a single fact, belief, or value, this is unusual. More commonly a number of facts, beliefs, and values are linked together to form a pattern, so it's important to gather all relevant data.

A. Things People Say Indicating Possible Resistance

Here are some things people say that indicate possible resistance to change, classified as facts, beliefs, and values:

1. Facts

a. "My doctor told me I shouldn't subject myself to too much stress."

b. "All my friends are in this department."

c. "I never had a course in accounting."

d. "That isn't in my job description."

e. "They just filed for bankruptcy."

f. "Other companies that buy supplies from them say they never deliver on time."

g. "You said you weren't going to make any more changes this year."

h. "The turnover rate is already 25% higher this year."

i. "We haven't received the training we were promised."

j. "Why should we do that? We haven't received a salary increase in three years."

2. Beliefs

a. "I'm too busy to do this."

b. "I'm a follower, not a leader."

c. "Yes, but…"

d. "He just tells people what they want to hear."

e. "He makes those changes just to harass us."

f. "He's more concerned with protecting his security than anything else."

g. "Watch out for him."

h. "In this company, it's not what you know but who you know that counts."

i. "Here we go again."

j. "That will never work here."

3. Values

a. "It's not important to me to have more authority."

b. "That's not on my list of priorities."

c. "It's essential that we're honest with each other."

d. "What you think really doesn't matter to me."

e. "Working with them is something I'd rather not do."

f. "Our mission should be…"

g. "What we need to emphasize is…"

h. "In the future, I'd like to see the organization…"

i. "We should be devoting more energy to…"

j. "Who cares what the goals are? I just do my job."

The Resistance Assessment Exercise can be used to provide people with hands-on experience in identifying the causes of resistance.

B. Common Causes of Resistance

Although there are many possible causes of resistance, in my experience the following eight reasons are the most common (Note: The Change Opinion Survey™ can be used to assess the extent to which these may be issues in changes you are planning):

1. **They believe the change process is being handled improperly.** When change is being proposed, people invariably have three questions: (1) Why? (2) How will it affect me? and (3) What's in it for me? Answering these questions effectively is crucial to preventing or minimizing resistance. Thomas Head (2000) said that resistance is usually caused by the change process (the how) instead of the intervention itself (the what). In addition to not having these questions answered, people resist change when they didn't have any input into the decision, they didn't like how the change was introduced, the change was a surprise, the timing of the change was bad, or they felt manipulated or deceived by management. People react to things like this with anger and resentment, because the methods used go against their values and violate their need for respect. We live in an age when employees expect to have their views considered, and to be treated with dignity. Therefore, people should be asked for input if:

a. They will be affected by the change.

b. You need their commitment to implement the change.

c. They have information or ideas to contribute.

d. They expect to be involved.

e. They could learn from the experience.

f. You want to expand or strengthen your base of support.

When initiating change, it's important to identify rewards that relate to employee's values—money, benefits, and new opportunities, for example—and build them into the change process, so they'll have a greater sense of ownership. People will be much more likely to support the change and help make it work, if there's something in it for them.

2. **They believe there isn't any need for the change.** Beckhard and Harris (1987) suggested that the degree of resistance is related to three factors: level of dissatisfaction with the status quo, desirability of the perceived change, and the practicality of the change. One of the most common causes of resistance is that people are content with the way things are now—if it's not broken, don't fix it. As long as this is true, change will only be viewed as unnecessary or negative.

Sometimes change is needed to avoid or escape a harmful situation. Some examples are bankruptcy, a hostile take over, or a decline in market share, profit, revenue, productivity, quality, morale, competitive position, and so on. A lot of the changes being introduced in American organizations now are in response to increased competition from other countries. Leaders maintain these changes are necessary to survive, but a lot of employees simply don't believe this, since they can't literally "see" the competition. Many of these employees are in denial, and need to face reality or be left behind.

3. **They believe the change will make it harder for them to meet their needs.** As such, they believe the change will make things worse, rather than make things better. Brehm's (1966) research showed that people resist change that they believe represents a loss of personal choice. In situations like these, facts tend to be less significant than the beliefs (assumptions, conclusions, and predictions) derived from them. For example, when managers talk about making the work more "efficient," employees often interpret this to mean that they will be doing more work. Also, if a change is presented as making the work easier, employees worry about positions being eliminated. Such concerns must be addressed to gain support for change. It's natural for people to think about how they're going to be affected by change, but unviable beliefs about bad things happening are damaging, because they are often based on inaccurate, incomplete, or mistaken information. These beliefs lead to fear, and values that emphasize protecting oneself against the perceived threat.

While it seems like ancient history now, this was one of the main reasons people resisted learning computers. Protesting that computers would make their work harder rather than easier, they continued using conventional equipment until they had to choose between becoming computer literate and being unemployed. For many of these people, claiming that computers would make their work harder was actually only an excuse to cover up their fear of the new technology.

4. **They believe the risks outweigh the benefits.** People are simultaneously motivated to meet their needs and to prevent bad things from happening, so accurately anticipating or predicting the probable outcomes of their actions is extremely important. Since we can never be absolutely sure how our actions will turn out, there's risk associated with everything we do. There's risk in change, but there's also risk in not changing ("What will happen if I change?" "What will happen if I don't change?"). Staying the same doesn't make people immune from risk. Nevertheless, people vary greatly in the degree of risk they perceive in a situation. Some people see gloom and doom around every corner, while others see a silver lining. In a team meeting where members are discussing a possible change, some may see a great deal of risk, while others may see little or no risk. The discussion can turn to conflict, as members assert their competing perspectives.

As shown in Figure 5.1, the Belief Continuum, the degree of perceived risk can range from none at all to extremely high. When contemplating change, an appropriate degree of concern is necessary to avoid mistakes, but people are capable of either underestimating or overestimating risks. Those who underestimate risks often regret their action, while those who overestimate risks often regret their inaction. It's natural for people to consider the worse case scenario, if only briefly. It can become a serious problem, however, if people treat the worse case scenario as an imminent reality, when the probability of its occurrence is remote.

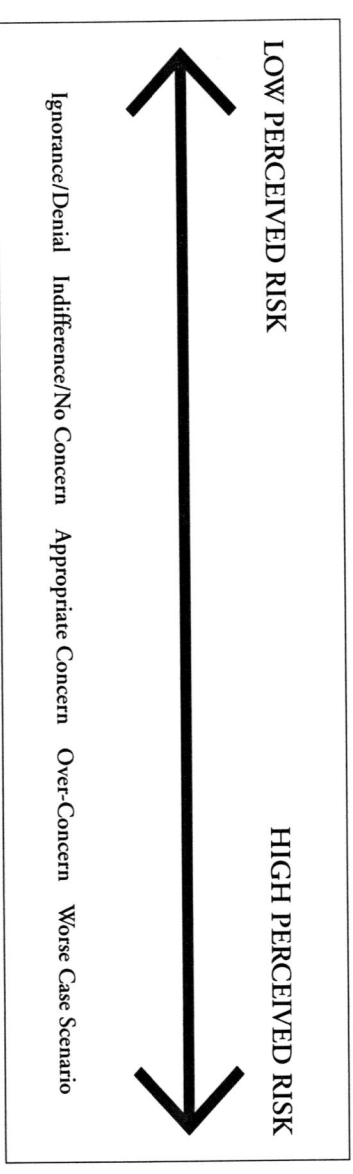

Figure 5.1
Belief Continuum

LOW PERCEIVED RISK   HIGH PERCEIVED RISK

Ignorance/Denial   Indifference/No Concern   Appropriate Concern   Over-Concern   Worse Case Scenario

To avoid either underestimating or overestimating risks, it's essential to have accurate facts and viable beliefs. Effective risk management, contingency plans, and feasibility studies would be impossible without such data. Inaccurate facts and unviable beliefs undermine efforts to plan and implement change. People who underestimate risks ignore relevant concerns, while those who overestimate risks will have too much concern. Either way, organizational growth is hindered.

In a cost/benefit analysis facts are actual costs, beliefs are anticipated costs, and benefits are values. Expectancy theory hold that people will be motivated when they believe that they can perform at the level necessary to attain rewards, and that these rewards are worthwhile (Lawler, 1973; Vroom, 1964). Something is only a benefit to people if it relates to their values. If people really want something, they'll be willing to pay more for it (actual cost), and take more risks to get it (anticipated cost). Figure 5.2 presents the following four scenarios, which describe the interplay between facts, beliefs and values in a cost/benefit analysis:

Figure 5.2
Cost/Benefit Analysis of Change

Perceived Benefit of Change

	LOW	HIGH
LOW	(a) Low Cost, Low Benefit	(b) Low Cost, High Benefit
HIGH	(c) High Cost, Low Benefit	(d) High Cost, High Benefit

Actual &
Perceived Cost of
Change

a. **Low cost and low benefit.** The expected reaction here is indifference. Under these conditions, the perceived benefit would have to be increased in order to generate any interest in change.

b. **Low cost and high benefit.** Conditions are favorable for change to take place.

c. **High cost and low benefit.** Resistance to change can be expected. To foster change under these conditions, the perceived benefit would have to be increased to justify the high cost.

d. **High cost and high benefit.** These conditions typically result in an approach-avoidance conflict. The decision to change would be difficult, as people weigh the high costs against the high benefits. In such situations, there's no substitute for accurate facts and viable beliefs.

5. **They believe they lack the ability to make the change.** When people learn about a proposed change, one of the things they invariably ask themselves is, "Will I be able to do this?" Lack of ability may appear to be resistance, but inability and unwillingness are quite different. Whereas resistance represents an unwillingness or un-receptiveness to change, inability to change stems from lack of knowledge, skills, confidence and/or necessary resources. *Knowledge* and *skills* have to do with one's actual ability, whereas *confidence* has to do with one's perceived ability. If people believe they can do something, they're more willing to try it; however, when they don't believe they can do it fear of failure increases their resistance. It's possible for people to possess the ability to change but still not believe that they can. In many cases, this belief becomes a self-fulfilling prophecy.

Resources can be divided into two categories: working conditions and communication. Working conditions are largely concerned with the availability and allocation of such physical resources as staff, money, time, equipment and supplies; communication has to do with the interpersonal environment on the job, and concerns such things as the effectiveness of supervision, feedback, cooperation, encouragement, support, and the information one receives. People can have the knowledge, skills, and confidence, but still be unable to make a change due to lack of necessary resources.

As Figure 5.3 indicates if we take into consideration both willingness and ability to change, four scenarios can be distinguished.

Figure 5.3
Willingness and Ability to Change

	Willing to Change	Unwilling to Change
Able to Change	(a) Both willing and able to change	(b) Able but unwilling to change
Unable to Change	(c) Willing but unable to change	(d) Both unwilling and unable to change

a. **Both willing and able to change.** In this scenario, the person both wants to change and can change. This is the combination most clearly associated with readiness to change.

b. **Able but unwilling to change.** In this scenario, the person can change but for some reason doesn't want to. This is the combination most clearly associated with resistance to change.

c. **Willing but unable to change.** In this scenario, the person wants to change but can't. In other words, the person lacks the knowledge, skills, confidence and/or resources necessary. Under this set of conditions, it's important to find out specifically why the person can't change or doesn't believe he/she can change, so that appropriate corrective measures can be taken. I've known managers who wanted to make the transition from a traditional hierarchical structure to a flatter, team-based structure, but they were so used to acting like a boss that they had difficulty sharing control. Some of them succeeded after considerable effort, while others failed in spite of everything they tried.

d. **Both unwilling and unable to change.** In this scenario, the person neither wants to change nor can change. This combination poses an interesting challenge diagnostically. It's important to determine if the person is really unwilling *and* unable to change. Sometimes people say they can't change when they just don't want to change. They would still resist the change, even if you helped them gain the necessary knowledge, skills, confidence, and/or resources ("I would if I could, but I can't so I won't"). In other cases people are openly critical of a change but the real issue, which often remains hidden, is that they don't believe they can do it. Finally, people might want to change if they were able to. Helping them gain the necessary knowledge, skills, confidence, and/or resources, therefore, could produce readiness to change. In my work with organizations moving to self-directed teams, I've also encountered people who could make the change but don't want to, often because they don't believe this is an effective way to manage. These people either resist the change or take a job where they can continue operating as they have in the past.

6. **They believe the change will fail.** People can resist change because they don't have confidence it will work, or they don't believe the resources are available to implement the change successfully. The anxiety stemming from these concerns will make it more difficult for people to support the change effort.

When people believe that the change will fail, it's important to make sure that they aren't overestimating the risks. Also, as stated above, sometimes when people are afraid that they might not be able to make a change, they cover this up by insisting that the change won't work. You can usually tell there's an underlying issue, because they argue against the change no matter what you say. In cases like this, probing beneath the surface to get at the real issue is necessary to deal with their resistance.

7. **They believe the change is inconsistent with their values.** Since values represent people's beliefs about what's important, they feel alienated if they believe the change conflicts with those values. Building greater compatibility between employee and organizational values is crucial to gaining commitment to change, and preventing or minimizing resistance.

8. **They believe those responsible for the change can't be trusted.** People will resist change if they believe that leadership either doesn't have their best interests at heart, or isn't being open and honest with them about the change and its impact. Lack of trust is an insidious and pervasive problem, robbing organizations out of much-needed commitment and performance. Just how big of an issue is mistrust? In a survey conducted by the Lausanne Institute, 91% of 474 government supervisors reported that lack of trust negatively impacts productivity. An *INC. Magazine* survey reported that 84% of employees don't trust their managers. Lack of trust puts people in a defensive posture. They spend their time protecting themselves from each other rather than focusing on organizational goals. If people have trouble trusting each other during routine times, this becomes an even greater issue during times of change.

Overcoming Resistance

The resistance strategy model, shown in Figure 5.4, is intended to take you step by step through a situation in which resistance is either anticipated or has already surfaced. The steps are as follows:

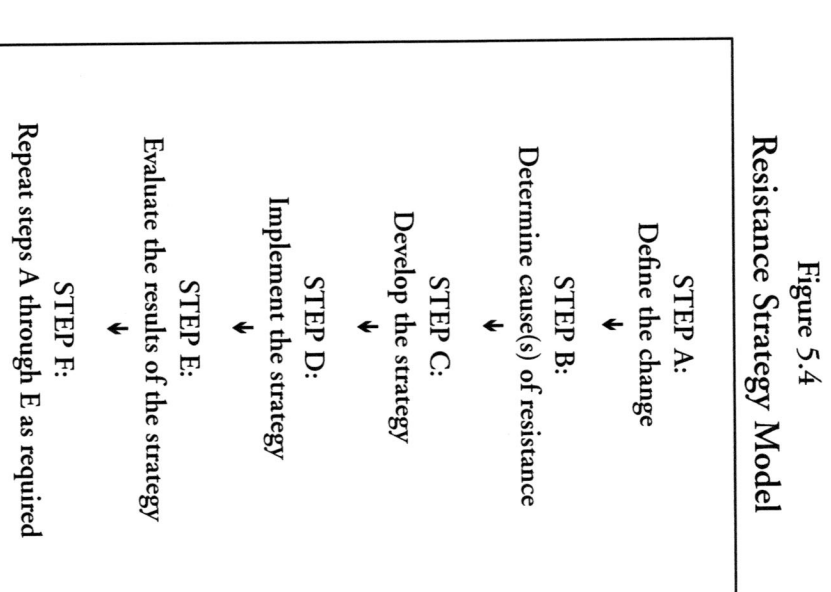

Figure 5.4
Resistance Strategy Model

STEP A:
Define the change

↓

STEP B:
Determine cause(s) of resistance

↓

STEP C:
Develop the strategy

↓

STEP D:
Implement the strategy

↓

STEP E:
Evaluate the results of the strategy

↓

STEP F:
Repeat steps A through E as required

A. Define the change. It's important to be as concrete, complete, and precise as possible in delineating what you want to change. When people state a desired change in vague or general terms, they often trigger resistance inadvertently. Another common mistake is to define the change only in terms of the *end* result. However, most changes involve a series of steps. In order to minimize resistance, therefore, it's important to define the steps as completely as possible. Otherwise, you may wrongly conclude that your goal is being resisted when in fact the problem may only be with one step, for which there is a viable alternative. The Current and Desired Organizational Beliefs, Values, and Behaviors Exercise at the end of this chapter can be used to help define change.

B. **Determine cause(s) of resistance.** After defining the intended change, determine who will be affected by the change and anticipate how they will respond to it. Ideally, you will be able to anticipate resistance in advance and take steps to prevent it. If resistance can't be prevented entirely, the next most desirable outcome is to minimize it.

Recall that resistance can stem from one or a combination of facts, beliefs, and values. Like putting together puzzle pieces, the more evidence you can gather from what people do and say, the better you will be able to separate causes from symptoms and develop strategies dealing with causes. Since you must infer facts, beliefs, and values from what people do and say, collect as much evidence as possible before drawing inferences. It's also important to regard your inferences as hypotheses, open to modification if additional information comes to light.

C. **Develop the strategy.** After identifying the cause(s) of resistance, the next step is to develop a strategy to deal with it. There's no magic formula for dealing with resistance. Even if your strategy is well thought out, something can always go wrong. Every situation is unique, and human behavior is too complex to predict with certainty. For any given instance of resistance, there will usually be a number of possible alternatives. Try to be as creative as possible in developing alternatives, so that you don't prematurely rule out one that might be effective.

Overcoming resistance is essentially a process of impacting people's facts, beliefs, feelings, values, and behavior. Some methods for dealing with facts and beliefs are to verify facts, clarify beliefs, challenge unviable beliefs, and suggest more viable beliefs. Examples of what you can ask or say to do these things are given in Table 5.2.

Since feelings are primarily consequences of thinking, they can't be changed through direct intervention. It doesn't do any good to say to someone, "Don't feel that way." Instead, changes in feelings result from changes in facts and beliefs. Nevertheless, when feelings surface, it's very important to acknowledge and clarify them. Some ways of doing these things are listed in Table 5.3.

When resistance relating to values is encountered, some methods for impacting them are to clarify values, challenge unviable values, and suggest more viable values. Examples are presented in Table 5.4. Finally, some approaches for impacting what people do are to clarify behavior, challenge ineffective behavior, and suggest more effective behavior. Table 5.5 gives some examples.

In developing potential strategies, keep in mind that facts, beliefs, feelings, values, and behavior are interrelated. Change in one variable often has ripple effects, changing others as well. Thus, value change often leads to change in beliefs, feelings and behavior, belief change often leads to change in values, feelings and behavior, and so on. Here are some examples:

1. When people succeed at something they didn't believe they could do, this challenges them to reassess the accuracy of their beliefs. They are also likely to have a feeling of accomplishment, and perhaps even realign values to support the new behavior.

2. After people express their feelings about an upsetting change, they are often able to examine facts, beliefs and values more objectively. This also can prevent them from making an impulsive decision.

3. When people experience a value conflict (e.g. between being honest vs. being sensitive), feelings can inhibit their ability to act. Clarifying which value is more important can help them sort out their feelings and resolve the conflict.

At any given time a person will be more receptive to change in one variable than others. A common mistake is developing a strategy around a variable that is not receptive to change. It's a waste of time, for example, to try to change a person's value for security, if the person staunchly defends that value. Instead, it might be more effective to indicate that after the reorganization everyone will be expected to engage in more risk-taking behavior.

Table 5.2
Interventions Aimed At Facts and Beliefs

Verifying Facts	"What information are you basing that on?"
	"What facts do you have to back that up?"
	"Do you have all the facts?"
	"Are your facts accurate and complete?"
	"How do you know that's true?"
	"What additional data do you need?"
	"What evidence do you have?"
	"How did you arrive at that conclusion?"
	"How can you be sure?"
	"Do you need more information before making a decision?"
	"What are the costs?"
Clarifying Beliefs	"What do you think about that?"
	"What's your opinion?"
	"What do you think is the primary cause?"
	"If you tried that, what do you think will happen?"
	"Do you think that will work? Why/why not?"
	"What problems do you see with that?"
	"What do you think he will do?"
	"What are the consequences?"
	"What are the risks?"
	"What opportunities do you see?"
	"What alternatives can you think of?"
	"How can this problem be solved."
	"What conclusion have you reached?"

Challenging Unviable Beliefs	"Do your beliefs allow you to meet your needs?" "Could these facts be explained in any other way?" "What impact do those beliefs have on your feelings/priorities/actions?" "That's not how I see the situation." "What are the chances of that happening?" "How else could his behavior be interpreted?" "Another way of viewing that would be…" "The facts don't seem to support that conclusion."
Suggesting More Viable Beliefs	"A more accurate way of looking at that would be…" "The facts tend to support the opposite conclusion." "You believe you have no other choice. Let's explore that to see if it's really true." "Another way of interpreting that would be…" "This is how I see the situation."

Table 5.3
Interventions Aimed At Feelings

Acknowledging Feelings	"I can see you're upset, can we talk about it?" "You sound angry, tell me what happened." "You're feeling frustrated." "You're really worried about this." "I can feel a lot of tension in this room." "Even though his actions make you angry, you're afraid to say anything." "You're discouraged because you haven't been able to make more progress."
Clarifying Feelings	"How does that make you feel?" "What are you concerned about?" "It looks like something's bothering you. Do you want to tell me about it." "What impact do your feelings have on your thoughts/decisions/actions?" "I know what you think, but I'm not sure how you feel."

Table 5.4

Interventions Aimed At Values

Clarifying Values	"What's most important to you?" "What outcomes do you want to see from this change?" "What's your bottom line?" "How would you prefer to deal with this?" "What is your preference?" "What factors do you think we ought to consider?" "Which choice is most consistent with your criteria?" "What criteria should we use to evaluate alternatives?" "What are your priorities?" "What are the benefits?" "If you had to make a choice, which one would it be?" "It looks like you disagree about what's important." "What would that accomplish?" "What purpose would that serve?"
Challenging Unviable Values	"I don't think you can have it both ways." "That seems to be less important in organizations now." "Do your values allow you to meet your needs?" "What impact do your values have on your thoughts/feelings/actions?" "The feedback indicates that a lot of managers don't walk the talk." "Your values seem to clash with those of other team members."
Suggesting More Viable Values	"One approach might be to place more emphasis on cooperation." "I think creating greater employee ownership would help morale." "Maybe it's time to place a higher priority on gender equity." "There would be some real benefits to becoming more customer-focused."

Table 5.5

Interventions Aimed At Behavior

Clarifying Behavior	"How could you go about doing that?" "What's the first step?" "How could you develop a plan of action?" "That sounds like a good idea, what else could you try?" "What could you say to him" "Why don't we role play that." "After that, what could you do?" "We've talked about how much this situation bothers you. Now let's talk about how you can change it." "How could you go about resolving this conflict?" "You know where you want to go; how can you get there?"
Challenging Ineffective Behaviors	"Do your actions allow you to meet your needs?" "What happened when you did that?" "I'm not sure that will work." "How effective was that?" "I think that would make the situation worse." "I'm not sure that would help you accomplish your goal." "In my experience that tends to put people on the defensive." "It seems to me that would be contrary to your value for…"
Suggesting More Effective Behaviors	"Another way of dealing with that would be to…" "It might be more effective if you…" "Perhaps you could try…" "An alternative way of responding would be to say…" "One way to build more team cohesiveness would be to…" "Perhaps it would help if you expressed more appreciation."

To help you become more adept at developing strategies, here are some suggestions for dealing with the eight common causes of resistance discussed earlier:

1. **They believe the change process is being handled improperly:**

   a. Explain how the change will affect them.

   b. Ask for and listen to their concerns.

   c. Apologize for mistakes, or the issue will never go away.

   d. Provide additional information (not excuses), as needed.

e. Ask for suggestions, in order to avoid similar situations in the future.

f. Be honest about suggestions you can and cannot accept, and indicate why. People appreciate a straight answer.

g. Follow through on agreements reached to improve the situation. If people believe they've been given the brush off, it will make things much worse.

2. **They believe there isn't any need for the change:**

a. Explain why the change is necessary.

b. Provide facts about the current challenges confronting the organization.

c. Explain how the change will help the organization survive and grow.

d. Listen and respond to their issues and concerns.

e. Clarify misconceptions about the change.

f. Indicate how the change will allow them to meet their needs more effectively.

g. Determine if they're setting their sights too low.

h. Discover if they're holding back due to fear of losing something.

i. Appeal to their sense of challenge.

j. Ask for their support in making the change work.

3. **They believe the change will make it harder for them to meet their needs:**

a. Discover if their facts are accurate and complete.

b. Determine if their beliefs are based on accurate information.

c. Provide additional information to correct mistaken or inaccurate beliefs.

d. Offer more viable interpretations of the facts.

e. Listen and express understanding.

f. Ask them what positive results they think can come out of the change.

g. Suggest ways you could make the change easier for them.

h. Ask how you can help them implement the change.

i. Ask for suggestions on how to make the change work better.

j. Ask for alternatives to the change that might be more effective.

k. Follow through on agreements reached to improve the situation.

4. **They believe the costs outweigh the benefits:**

a. Ask them to discuss the costs.

b. Determine if the costs are based on accurate information.

c. Provide additional information to correct inaccurate or mistaken beliefs.

d. Offer more viable interpretations of the facts.

e. Listen and respond to their issues and concerns.

f. Specify the material rewards (money, benefits, etc.) they will receive from the change.

g. Point out how the benefits of the change relate to their values.

h. Ask them if they can think of additional benefits.

5. **They believe they lack the ability to make the change:**

a. Ask them to express their concerns.

b. Listen and respond with empathy.

c. Convey a willingness to work with the person.

d. Ask open questions to get at all relevant issues.

e. Probe for unexpressed concerns and invite dialogue.

f. Express confidence and reassurance.

g. Offer encouragement and support.

h. Make resources available (time, money, training, etc.).

i. Offer coaching/mentoring.

j. Follow-up on agreements.

k. Provide feedback on progress.

l. Keep channels of communication open.

6. **They believe the change will fail:**

a. Ask for and listen to their concerns.

b. Discover if their facts are accurate and complete.

c. Determine if their beliefs are based on accurate information.

d. Provide additional information to correct mistaken or inaccurate beliefs.

e. Offer more viable interpretations of the facts.

f. Ask for suggestions to help make the change successful.

g. Ask for alternatives to the change that might be more effective.

h. Ask how you can help them implement the change.

i. Encourage them to visualize positive outcomes.

j. Follow through on agreements reached to improve the situation.

k. Ask for their support in making the change work.

l. Express confidence in their ability to implement the change successfully.

7. **They believe the change is inconsistent with their values:**

a. Ask them to describe the inconsistencies they see between the change and their values.

b. Explore the inconsistencies to determine if they are perceived or real.

c. If the inconsistencies are perceived but not real, provide additional information as needed.

d. When the inconsistencies are real, acknowledge their concerns.

e. Ask for suggestions on how the problem can be resolved.

f. When possible, modify the change.

g. If the change can't be modified, be honest about it and ask for cooperation.

h. Build common ground.

i. Point out the benefits of the change (there are often more benefits than people realize).

j. Ask questions to determine if there are other issues involved, such as anxiety about the change or lack of confidence.

k. Offer your help and support during the change process.

8. **They believe those responsible for the change can't be trusted:**

a. Share information openly and directly.

b. Invite discussion of trust issues.

c. Listen and convey understanding.

d. Take responsibility for mistakes.

e. Walk the talk.

f. Follow through on agreements.

g. Resolve disagreements directly and in good faith.

h. Seek win-win outcomes.

i. Be consistent and sincere.

j. Honor confidential information.

k. Give others credit when it's due.

l. Involve others in decisions affecting them.

m. Avoid actions contributing to mistrust (gossip, blaming, etc.).

n. Act out of integrity and not expediency.

o. Ask how a climate of trust can be fostered and maintained.

D. Implement the strategy. In implementing a strategy, the two most important factors are *timing* and *pacing*. Timing has to do with when you implement the strategy. An adequate strategy may intensify resistance simply because it was introduced at the wrong time. On-going communication and feedback will help you determine the best time to implement a change.

Pacing, which is related to timing, concerns how much of your strategy to introduce at any given time. Even people receptive to change have limits to how much they can handle, since any change involves adjustment. If you push people, you could inadvertently create resistance that wasn't there. In their research, Kotter and Heskitt (1992) found that adaptive organizations focused on making incremental changes. Avoid defeating yourself by going too fast. If people show signs of anxiety, stress, or resentment, take a look at the pace of change. Since people will respond differently to your strategy, you may need to go slower with some of them. Also some people require a great deal of reassurance during times of change, while others don't seem to need any at all. Allowing for individual differences and modifying the pace accordingly will enhance the effectiveness of your strategy.

E. Evaluate the results of your strategy. Evaluating the effectiveness of your strategy is important in successfully dealing with resistance. Evaluation is not a one-time procedure that is completed after the strategy has been implemented. Rather, it is an ongoing process that begins from the moment you start implementing your strategy and continues until the resistance is reduced or eliminated. Throughout the implementation phase, what people do and say will tell you whether or not your strategy is working. Sometimes your attempts to deal with resistance will lead to dramatic results which are clearly positive or negative, but more often the results will show up in small changes. In their zeal to lower resistance, some people overlook or play down small changes, or even abandon good strategies if they don't meet with immediate success.

You can avoid this mistake by keeping in mind that even small change in beliefs, values, or behavior can be a significant sign that your strategy is working. Since these elements are interrelated, a tiny change may signify the beginning of a process that eventually yields tremendous results. Therefore notice *any* positive changes, regardless of magnitude, and nurture them to the fullest.

F. Repeat steps A through E, as required. Since any strategy is a hypothesis about how to lower resistance, you won't know if it's working until you begin implementing it. The results of your ongoing evaluation will tell you if you need to modify your approach. Rarely will you be able to develop and implement a strategy without making adjustments. Be prepared to encounter obstacles and to deal with them as needed. Some common mistakes are:

1. Incorrectly assessing resistance.

2. Basing your strategy on a symptom rather than on a cause of resistance.

3. Failing to consider all relevant factors in developing the strategy.

4. Implementing a strategy not well suited to the situation.

5. Failing to adjust the strategy to account for new information.

6. Implementing the strategy at the wrong time or at an unrealistic pace.

In addition, your strategy may have unanticipated consequences. It could backfire, causing more problems than you had originally. The cause of resistance may change in the middle of implementing your strategy, or people may respond with unanticipated counter measures. When faced with setbacks, therefore, repeat steps A through E as often as necessary to accomplish your objective. The biggest mistake is to stubbornly stick with a strategy, even when it's not working. You won't be able to overcome resistance in others if you resist changing an ineffective strategy!

"Two steps forward, one step back. Change and resistance, the ebb and flow of organizational life. Change is necessary for survival and growth, but change brings risks, and with risks, resistance. Managing change and resistance are essential skills in today's increasingly complex and competitive world. By implementing the concepts and techniques presented in this article, you can help your organization carve out a path to a successful future.

CHANGE OPINION SURVEY™

PURPOSE: To assess eight common causes of resistance to organizational change (40 items).

Procedures

The Change Opinion Survey™ can be administered prior to implementing change in order to prevent resistance, or after resistance begins to surface in order to minimize its impact. It can also be administered before and after a change, as a way of evaluating its implementation.

The instrument can be given to everyone involved with a change, or to a representative sample. The specific change being surveyed should be specified on the cover page of the instrument.

One way to use the data is to meet with those leading the change effort, display the completed Change Opinion Profile, and then facilitate a discussion of the reasons for resistance. Mean scores can range from 0 to 20. The higher a mean score, the more indication that a "common cause" is a reason for resistance. Mean scores above 14 indicate considerable resistance.

Following a discussion of causes, strategies can then be developed for overcoming resistance. Some suggestions can be found in the Overcoming Resistance, Develop the Strategy section of this article. The Plan for Implementing Organizational Change Exercise can be used to outline a complete change plan, including steps for overcoming resistance.

Change Opinion Survey™

by
Ken Hultman

Name:_____

Position:_____

Team/Department:_____

Date Completed:_____

Instructions

The purpose of the Change Opinion Survey™ is to give you an opportunity to state your views about the following organizational change:

_____

_____

Read each item on the next two pages and circle the response that best describes your opinion. The scale is a continuum from 0 to 4, with 0 meaning strongly disagree and 4 meaning strongly agree. Your responses will be combined with others in the organization and will be kept confidential. You will receive a summary of the results once they've been compiled.

THANK YOU FOR COMPLETING THIS SURVEY

please turn the page and begin ⟹

	Strongly Disagree				Strongly Agree
1. I didn't have any input into the change.	0	1	2	3	4
2. There isn't any need for the change.	0	1	2	3	4
3. The change makes it harder to get our work done.	0	1	2	3	4
4. The risks of the change outweigh the benefits.	0	1	2	3	4
5. I lack the knowledge and skills needed to make this change.	0	1	2	3	4
6. The change isn't going to work	0	1	2	3	4
7. The change emphasizes the wrong priorities.	0	1	2	3	4
8. They aren't telling us the real reason for the change.	0	1	2	3	4
9. The timing of the change is bad.	0	1	2	3	4
10. We're just jumping on the bandwagon with other organizations.	0	1	2	3	4
11. The change will lower productivity and morale.	0	1	2	3	4
12. The change is a big gamble.	0	1	2	3	4
13. I'm not sure I can do what's required of me.	0	1	2	3	4
14. The change sounds good in theory, but not in reality.	0	1	2	3	4
15. The change will take us in the wrong direction.	0	1	2	3	4
16. Management isn't being honest with us about the change.	0	1	2	3	4
17. The reasons for the change were never explained.	0	1	2	3	4
18. We can remain competitive without changing.	0	1	2	3	4
19. The change will do more harm than good.	0	1	2	3	4
20. The cost of the change can't be justified.	0	1	2	3	4
21. I lack confidence in my ability to make the change.	0	1	2	3	4
22. The conditions needed for the change to succeed are lacking.	0	1	2	3	4
23. I don't care about the change.	0	1	2	3	4
24. Those responsible for the change have a hidden agenda.	0	1	2	3	4
25. Management asked for our ideas, but then didn't use them.	0	1	2	3	4
26. We seem to change for the sake of change.	0	1	2	3	4
27. The change creates more hurdles to jump over.	0	1	2	3	4
28. I don't see anything good coming from this change.	0	1	2	3	4
29. Resources needed to make the change are lacking	0	1	2	3	4

		Strongly Disagree			Strongly Agree
30. We've tried changes like this before and they didn't work.	0	1	2	3	4
31. The change goes against my values.	0	1	2	3	4
32. Information about the change is being withheld from us.	0	1	2	3	4
33. The change is being implemented too quickly.	0	1	2	3	4
34. Most people can't see what the change will accomplish.	0	1	2	3	4
35. The change just adds to our workload.	0	1	2	3	4
36. The change is bad for business.	0	1	2	3	4
37. Communication about the change is lacking.	0	1	2	3	4
38. The change will last for a while, then we'll go back to the old way.	0	1	2	3	4
39. The change is distracting us from more important issues.	0	1	2	3	4
40. I don't trust the people making the change.	0	1	2	3	4

Calculating Scores

This instrument consists of 40 items, 5 pertaining to each of the eight "common causes" of resistance. A Change Opinion Profile can be developed by following these procedures:

(A). Total up the scores of each person completing the instrument for the eight causes. Items pertaining to each reason are:

1. They believe the change process is being handled improperly: 1, 9, 17, 25, 33
2. They believe there isn't any need for the change: 2, 10, 18, 26, 34
3. They believe the change will make it harder for them to meet their needs: 3, 11, 19, 27, 35
4. They believe the risks outweigh the benefits: 4, 12, 20, 28, 36
5. They believe they lack the ability to make the change: 5, 13, 21, 29, 37
6. They believe the change will fail: 6, 14, 22, 30, 38
7. The change is inconsistent with their values: 7, 15, 23, 31, 39
8. They believe those responsible for the change can't be trusted: 8, 16, 24, 32, 40

(B). Add the totals of all respondents together for each "common cause," and divide these totals by the number of respondents completing the instrument. This will give you the mean or average scores for this group of respondents.

(C). Place a dot at the corresponding point on the profile for the eight causes, and connect the dots with a line.

Change Opinion Profile

| | Openness to Change |
| Resistance to Change |

Respondents Believe:

The change process is being handled improperly.

There isn't any need for the change.

The change will make it harder for them to meet their needs.

The risks outweigh the benefits.

They lack the ability to make the change.

The change will fail.

The change is inconsistent with their values.

Those responsible for the change can't be trusted.

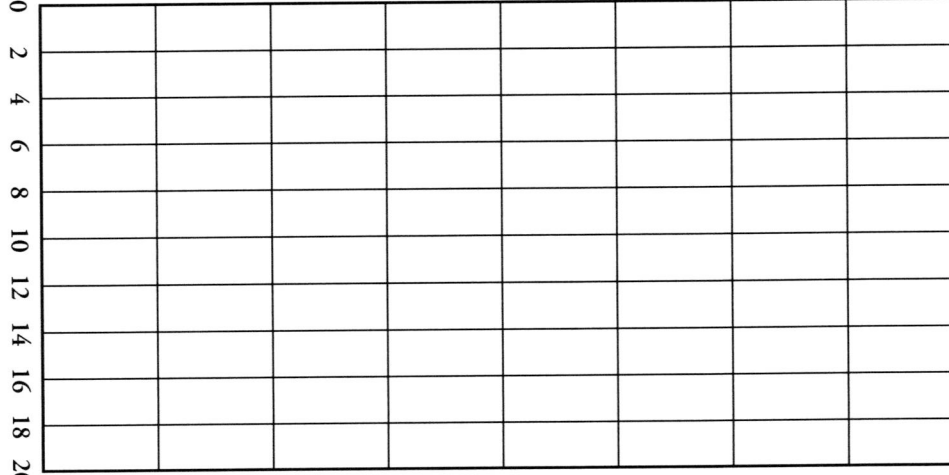

MEAN SCORES

0 2 4 6 8 10 12 14 16 18 20

RESISTANCE ASSESSMENT EXERCISE

PURPOSE: To provide hands-on experience in assessing resistance to organizational change.

Procedure

- EXPLAIN that participants will now have an opportunity to assess resistance.

- HAND OUT a copy of the Resistance Assessment Exercise worksheet to each participant, and GIVE these instructions:

  Think of an example of someone you work with who resists change.

  In the space provided on the worksheet, indicate what the person does and says to show resistance. Try to identify the resistance pattern by categorizing what the person says into facts, beliefs, feelings and values.

  Then indicate your initial diagnosis, what additional information you need to confirm the diagnosis, and what questions you will ask to gather this information.

- GIVE participants 15 minutes to complete the exercise.

- ASK participants to share their examples with the whole group.

- PROVIDE feedback to participants and ASK them to give each other feedback.

Resistance Assessment Exercise

WHAT DOES THE PERSON DO?

WHAT DOES THE PERSON SAY?

Facts

Beliefs

Feelings

Values

What is your initial assessment of the cause of resistance?

What additional information do you need to confirm the assessment?

What questions will you ask to gather this information?

CURRENT AND DESIRED ORGANIZATIONAL BELIEFS, VALUES, AND BEHAVIORS

PURPOSE: To clarify current organizational beliefs, values and behaviors, and decide what organizational beliefs, values and behavior people desire in the future. It is intended to take one hour.

Procedure

* EXPLAIN that before initiating organizational change, it's important to know where you are now and where you'd like to go.

* DIVIDE participants into subgroups of 4-6.

* HAND OUT a copy of the Current/Desired worksheets to each participant, and GIVE these instructions:

  I'd like one subgroup to list on a flip chart the beliefs, values and behaviors of people in the organization currently.

  I'd like the other subgroup to list on a flip chart the beliefs, values and behaviors you'd like to see in the future.

  (Note: If you have more than 2 subgroups, ASSIGN half of the subgroups to work on the "current" and the other half to work on the "desired.")

* GIVE the subgroups 15 minutes to complete their lists.

* ASK each subgroup to share their results with the whole group, starting with the "current" subgroup(s).

* DISCUSS the results with the whole group:

  What differences do you see?

  What needs to happen to get from the "current" to the "desired"?

  What obstacles could get in the way of the desired changes?

* ASK for and RESPOND to questions.

CURRENT

Beliefs

Values

Behaviors

DESIRED

<u>Beliefs</u>

<u>Values</u>

<u>Behaviors</u>

PLAN FOR IMPLEMENTING ORGANIZATIONAL CHANGE

PURPOSE: To develop a plan of action for initiating organizational change.

Procedure

Participants should bring with them any relevant information that will help them plan an organizational change, such as work done on the *Current and Desired Organizational Values, Beliefs, and Behaviors Exercise,* or other exercises included in this book. This exercise is intended to take three hours.

- HAND OUT a copy of the Change Planning Guide to each participant, and ASK them to complete it individually:

  Think of a change you'd like to make in your organization and develop a plan of action for implementing that change.

  As you address the questions on the Change Planning Guide, keep in mind that any change means that people's behavior will be different. That's the only way you can determine if your change has been implemented successfully. Therefore, (1) start by describing the changes you want to make, (2) next indicate the ways people's values, beliefs and behaviors will need to be different to support your change, (3) then identify how you can bring about your changes and, finally, (4) indicate what you can do to prevent or minimize resistance.

- GIVE participants about 30 minutes to complete the Change Planning Guide individually.

- DIVIDE participants into subgroups of 4 people each and GIVE these instructions:

  Each person should take turns sharing the information of their Change Planning Guide with the subgroup.

  Subgroup members should give each other feedback and suggestions.

  Take 15 minutes to focus on each person, so you can finish in one hour.

- ASK individuals to share the information on their Change Planning Guide with the whole group, and PROVIDE feedback and suggestions, as appropriate.

- ALLOW 60 minutes for this large group discussion.

- DEBRIEF key learning points with the whole group.

CHANGE PLANNING GUIDE

1. **What changes do you want to make?**

2. **In what ways will people's values, beliefs and behaviors need to be different to support your change?**

3. **How can you bring about these changes?**

Where will you start (need, think, feel, decide, or do)?

How will you communicate your vision for the change to others?

How will you gain acceptance for the change?

Who will you involve in the change decision and how?

What additional information do you need and how do you plan to get it?

What additional resources (staff, time, money, equipment, etc.) do you need?

What is your implementation plan and timetable?

How will you monitor progress?

4. **What kind of resistance do you expect and what can you do to prevent or minimize it?**

6

BUILDING AN ADAPTIVE ORGANIZATION

Purpose: To assess an organization's current and desired operating practices, and to determine how it can become more adaptive to changing conditions. Also includes supplemental guidelines for values-driven decision-making, problem-solving, conflict resolution, and strategic planning.

Introduction

The ability of an organization to adapt to changing conditions is essential to success in the new economy. In *Corporate Culture and Performance*, Kotter and Heskett (1992) conclude from their extensive research on corporate culture that organizations won't be able to sustain excellent performance over the long haul unless they have values allowing them to change and adapt. In *Built to Last: Successful Habits of Visionary Companies*, Collins and Porras (1994) boil the extraordinary success of 18 visionary companies down to one key principle: preserving the core ideology (mission and values) while stimulating change in culture, operating practices, goals, and strategies. Similarly, in *The Living Company: Habits for Survival in a Turbulent Business Environment*, Arie De Geus (1997) reports that long-lived companies have values that allow them to anticipate the need to adapt and change. Organizations that hold on to outmoded thinking and practices will be left behind by those that are more flexible and nimble.

An *adaptive* organization is one that modifies business practices in response to the changing needs of its stakeholders: customers, employees, and stockholders. It takes strong leadership to create and maintain an adaptive organization, because practices that become part of corporate culture and tradition tend to resist change. The Adaptive Organization Scale™ allows you to work with a team to address two questions: (1) *What kind of organization are we currently,* and (2) *How can we become more adaptive?*

Procedures

Give a copy of the Adaptive Organization Scale to team members and ask them to complete it. This should be done prior to a team session scheduled to present and discuss results. The Scale is divided into two parts. *Part 1: Operating Practices*, uses a continuum extending from strongly collaborative to strongly directive to help an organization identify how it is functioning currently and how it would prefer to function in the six areas of Decision-Making, Communication, Roles, Structures, Rewards and Leadership Style (see Figure 6.1, which operationally defines the operating practices). *Part 2: Potential Barriers*, assesses five common obstacles to establishing and maintaining an adaptive culture: Morale, Trust, Conflict, Listening, and Job

Security (Note: the Scale can be supplemented by interview data focusing on organizational strengths and areas needing improvement).

Calculate scores for Part 1 and Part 2 using the instructions provided and complete an Adaptive Organization Profile for the team. At a team meeting, give each member a completed copy of the Profile and discuss:

(a) The similarities and differences between current and desired operating practices,

(b) How to move from current to desired practices, and

(c) How to deal with any potential barriers to becoming a more adaptive organization.

The team should define specifically how the organization can become more adaptive and leave with a detailed plan of action, indicating who will do what and by when. Follow-up meetings should also be held to discuss progress and resolve issues.

Figure 6.1
Operating Practices Continuum

COLLABORATIVE⟸   ⟹DIRECTIVE

	Strongly Collaborative	Collaborative Emphasis	Combination	Emphasis Directive	Directive Strongly
Decision-Making	Almost all decisions are made by teams. Emphasis is on empowerment and creativity	Most decisions are made by teams.	Decisions are made my teams or management on a case by case basis	Most decisions are made by management. Input from others is usually sought beforehand.	Almost all decisions are made by management. Emphasis is on following orders, conformity, and regimentation.
Communication	There are no constraints on communication.	Emphasis is primarily on face-to-face communication (personal).	A combination of face-to-face and written communication is used.	Emphasis is primarily on written communication (impersonal).	Communication is top-down, with a strong emphasis on documentation.
Roles	No arbitrary distinctions are made between people based on formal roles. People are utilized because of their abilities.	Emphasis is primarily on utilizing people because of their abilities.	People are utilized based on a combination of their abilities and their position.	Emphasis is primarily on utilizing people because of their position.	Roles are defined by job descriptions. People are utilized because of their position (title, status, and seniority).

COLLABORATIVE⇐

⇒DIRECTIVE

	Strongly Collaborative	Collaborative Emphasis	Combination	Emphasis Directive	Directive Strongly
Structures	People are encouraged to develop informal networks. Formal structures are seen as barriers to empowerment.	Emphasis is on informal networks.	A combination of informal networks and formal structures is used.	Emphasis is primarily on formal structures.	Structures are formal and hierarchical. Emphasis is on following the chain-of-command.
Rewards	Rewards are based on team performance.	Rewards are based primarily on team performance.	Rewards are based on a combination of individual and team performance.	Rewards are based primarily on individual performance.	Rewards are based exclusively on individual performance.
Leadership Style	Strong emphasis is placed on relationships; process-focus.	Emphasis is placed primarily on relationships.	A combination of relationships and task-completion is stressed.	Emphasis is primarily on task-completion.	Strong emphasis is placed on task completion; results-focus.

ADAPTIVE ORGANIZATION SCALE

Directions: The Scale is divided into two parts. Part 1, *Operating Practices*, asks you to compare current with desired practices in six key areas: Decision-Making, Communication, Roles, Structures, Rewards, and Leadership Style. Part 2, *Potential Barriers*, asks you to evaluate the organization in five areas that can prevent it from becoming more adaptive: Morale, Trust, Conflict, Listening with Understanding, and Job Security. Your responses will be combined with others in the organization and will remain anonymous. You will receive a summary of the results.

Part 1: Operating Practices

For each of the following six areas read the responses and (1) place an X in the box next to the one that best describes how your organization functions currently, and (2) place an X in the box next to the one that best describes how you would prefer to see your organization function (Note: if desired, you could select the same response for both current and desired).

Decision-Making

	Current (Select one)	Desired (Select one)
1. Almost all decisions are made by teams.	☐	☐
2. Most decisions are made by teams.	☐	☐
3. Decisions are sometimes made by teams and sometimes by management.	☐	☐
4. Most decisions are made by management.	☐	☐
5. Almost all decisions are made by management. Emphasis is on following orders, conformity, and regimentation.	☐	☐

Communication

	Current (Select one)	Desired (Select one)
1. There are no constraints on communication.	☐	☐
2. Emphasis is primarily on face-to-face communication (personal). Few barriers to upward communication exist.	☐	☐
3. A combination of face-to-face and written communication is used. Some barriers to upward communication exist.	☐	☐

Communication

	Current (Select one)	Desired (Select one)
4. Emphasis is primarily on written communication (impersonal). Many barriers to upward communication exist.	☐	☐
5. Communication is top-down, with a strong emphasis on written, formal documentation.	☐	☐

Roles

	Current (Select one)	Desired (Select one)
1. No arbitrary distinctions are made between people based on formal roles. People are utilized because of their abilities.	☐	☐
2. Emphasis is primarily on utilizing people because of their abilities.	☐	☐
3. People are utilized based on a combination of their abilities and their formal position.	☐	☐
4. Emphasis is primarily on utilizing people because of their formal position.	☐	☐
5. Roles are defined by job descriptions. People are utilized because of their formal position (title, status, seniority).	☐	☐

Structures

	Current (Select one)	Desired (Select one)
1. People are encouraged to develop and utilize informal networks. Formal structures are viewed as barriers to empowerment.	☐	☐
2. Emphasis is on informal networks.	☐	☐
3. A combination of informal networks and formal structures is used.	☐	☐
4. Emphasis is primarily on formal structures.	☐	☐
5. Structures are formal and hierarchical. Emphasis is on following the chain-of-command.	☐	☐

Rewards

	Current (Select one)	Desired (Select one)
1. Rewards are based on team performance.	☐	☐
2. Rewards are based primarily on team performance.	☐	☐
3. Rewards are based on a combination of team and individual performance.	☐	☐
4. Rewards are based primarily on individual performance.	☐	☐
5. Rewards are based exclusively on individual performance.	☐	☐

Leadership Style

	Current (Select one)	Desired (Select one)
1. Strong emphasis is placed on relationships; process-focus.	☐	☐
2. Emphasis is placed primarily on relationships.	☐	☐
3. A combination of relationships and task-completion is used.	☐	☐
4. Emphasis is placed primarily on task-completion.	☐	☐
5. Strong emphasis is placed on task-completion; results-focus.	☐	☐

Part 2: Potential Barriers

Think about the following statements as they apply to your organization currently, and circle the response that best reflects your opinion.

Morale

	Strongly Disagree				Strongly Agree
1. Employees are treated as persons, not numbers.	0	1	2	3	4
2. Morale is high.	0	1	2	3	4
3. People's contributions are given proper recognition.	0	1	2	3	4
4. People show respect for each other.	0	1	2	3	4
5. There's very little grumbling and complaining.	0	1	2	3	4

Trust

	Strongly Disagree				Strongly Agree
1. People have each other's best interests at heart.	0	1	2	3	4
2. People don't play politics to get what they want.	0	1	2	3	4
3. People follow through on commitments.	0	1	2	3	4
4. People don't have hidden agendas.	0	1	2	3	4
5. People trust each other.	0	1	2	3	4

Conflict

	Strongly Disagree				Strongly Agree
1. Competition between people is low.	0	1	2	3	4
2. People take responsibility for mistakes.	0	1	2	3	4
3. People agree to disagree.	0	1	2	3	4
4. People seek win-win outcomes.	0	1	2	3	4
5. People work together to resolve conflicts.	0	1	2	3	4

Listening with Understanding

	Strongly Disagree				Strongly Agree
1. Misunderstandings seldom occur.	0	1	2	3	4
2. Information is shared openly and freely.	0	1	2	3	4
3. People take time to build relationships.	0	1	2	3	4
4. People feel free to express their ideas and opinions.	0	1	2	3	4
5. People try to listen and understand each other.	0	1	2	3	4

Job Security

	Strongly Disagree				Strongly Agree
1. People don't worry about losing their job.	0	1	2	3	4
2. People's jobs aren't held over their head like a club.	0	1	2	3	4
3. If you do competent work, you can be reasonably sure of keeping your job.	0	1	2	3	4
4. People don't spend time protecting their turf.	0	1	2	3	4
5. It's not who you know but what you know that counts.	0	1	2	3	4

Calculate Scores and Complete the Adaptive Organization Profile

(a) Part 1: Operating Procedures Bar Graphs

- For each operating practice (Decision-Making, Communication, Roles, Structures, Rewards, and Leadership Style), respondents select from among five alternatives to reflect their opinion regarding CURRENT and DESIRED practices. Calculate the percent (%) of team members that checked each of the five alternatives for both CURRENT and DESIRED. For example, if ten people completed the Scale and in the Decision-Making category eight of them checked the fifth alternative under CURRENT (Almost all decisions are made by management), that would be 80% of respondents.

- On Part 1 of the Profile, complete bar graphs for each operating practice, using the height of each bar to reflect CURRENT and DESIRED percentages. Use different shading for CURRENT and DESIRED bars so they can be distinguished more clearly.

(b) Part 2: Potential Barriers Line Graph

- Add the totals of all respondents together for each of the five variables (Morale, Trust, Conflict, Listening, Job Security),

- Divide these scores by the number of respondents completing the Scale (this will give you the average or mean score for each variable),

- Place a dot at the corresponding point on Part 2 of the Profile for each variable, and

- Connect the dots with a line.

Adaptive Organization Profile

Organization/Team _____

N=_____

Part 1: Operating Practices Bar Graphs

DECISION-MAKING

100%					
90%					
80%					
70%					
60%					
50%					
40%					
30%					
20%					
10%					

Current	Desired	Current	Desired	Current	Desired	Current	Desired	Current	Desired
Strongly Collaborative		Collaborative Emphasis		Combination		Directive Emphasis		Strongly Directive	

COMMUNICATION

100%					
90%					
80%					
70%					
60%					
50%					
40%					
30%					
20%					
10%					

Current	Desired	Current	Desired	Current	Desired	Current	Desired	Current	Desired
Strongly Collaborative		Collaborative Emphasis		Combination		Directive Emphasis		Strongly Directive	

ROLES

		Strongly Collaborative		Collaborative Emphasis		Combination		Directive Emphasis		Strongly Directive	
		Current	Desired	Current	Desired	Current	Desired	Current	Desired	Current	Desired

100%
90%
80%
70%
60%
50%
40%
30%
20%
10%

STRUCTURES

		Strongly Collaborative		Collaborative Emphasis		Combination		Directive Emphasis		Strongly Directive	
		Current	Desired	Current	Desired	Current	Desired	Current	Desired	Current	Desired

100%
90%
80%
70%
60%
50%
40%
30%
20%
10%

REWARDS

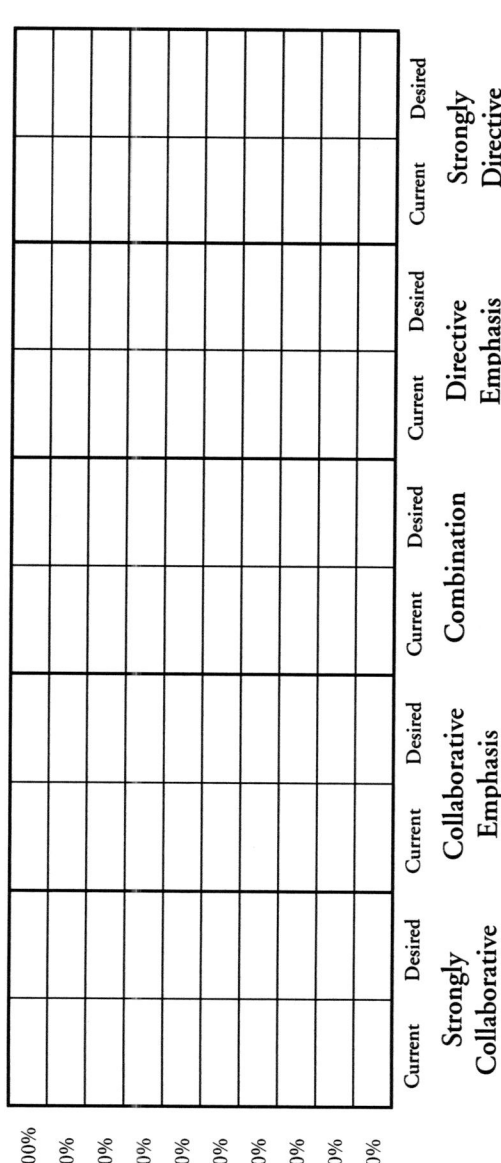

	Strongly Collaborative		Collaborative Emphasis		Combination		Directive Emphasis		Strongly Directive	
	Current	Desired	Current	Desired	Current	Desired	Current	Desired	Current	Desired
100%										
90%										
80%										
70%										
60%										
50%										
40%										
30%										
20%										
10%										

LEADERSHIP STYLE

	Strongly Collaborative		Collaborative Emphasis		Combination		Directive Emphasis		Strongly Directive	
	Current	Desired	Current	Desired	Current	Desired	Current	Desired	Current	Desired
100%										
90%										
80%										
70%										
60%										
50%										
40%										
30%										
20%										
10%										

Part 2: Potential Barriers Line Graph

	Morale	Trust	Conflict	Listening	Job Security
Excellent 4					
3.5					
Good 3					
2.5					
Fair 2					
1.5					
Poor 1					
0.5					
0					

Supplemental Guidelines

To facilitate the embedding of organizational values, this section included detailed guidelines for the following:

- Values-Driven Decision-Making
- Values-Driven Problem-Solving
- Values Driven Conflict Resolution
- Values-Driven Strategic Planning

STEPS FOR VALUES-DRIVEN DECISION-MAKING

a. What decision needs to be made?

b. How is the decision related to vision or goals?

c. What value(s) will be affected by the decision?

d. Who should be involved in making the decision? (How many of those affected by the decision or required for its implementation should be involved?)

e. What information relevant to this decision is available? Is additional information needed? If so, how will it be gathered?

f. What alternatives are available?

g. Which alternative is most consistent with the associated value(s)?

h. How will the decision be implemented? *Who* will do *what* and by *when*?

i. How will you follow-up to evaluate the decision?

STEPS FOR VALUES-DRIVEN PROBLEM-SOLVING

a. What is the problem? Who should be involved in defining the problem?

b. How does it relate to vision or goals?

c. What value(s) is impacted by the problem?

d. Who should be involved in solving the problem, and answering the following questions?

e. What are the symptoms of the problem?

f. What are the consequences of the symptoms?

g. What is causing the symptoms?

h. What potential solutions are there for dealing with the causes?

i. Which solution(s) are most consistent with the associated values?

j. How can the solution be implemented? *Who* will do *what* and by *when*?

k. How will you follow-up to evaluate the solution(s)?

STEPS FOR VALUES-DRIVEN CONFLICT RESOLUTION

When someone has an issue with you:

1. Seek to understand the conflict from the other person's point of view.

   a. Define the nature of the conflict.

   b. Specify the value(s) impacted by the conflict.

   c. Clarify the issues by:

   Asking for details

   "What did I do to upset you?"

   "Can you be more specific?"

   "Can you give me an example?"

   "Tell me more about…"

   "Is there anything else you want to tell me?"

   Check understanding

   "Are you saying…?

   "Do you mean…?"

   "I'm confused about…"

   "I'm not sure what you mean by…"

   Summarize

   "So what you're saying is…?"

   "Let me make sure I've got this right…"

   "Let me summarize."

   "So far you've said…"

   d. Reflect both the content and feeling expressed by the other person (this indicates that you hear and understand the other person, not that you agree with him or her).

   "You were hurt when I didn't comment on your remarks at the meeting."

   "When I expressed concerns about the project, you felt I was criticizing your work."

   "You're frustrated because you don't feel like you're getting ahead."

   "I can see you're very upset by my actions."

   "You feel this incident has damaged our working relationship."

2. After the other person feels heard, you have earned the right to give your point of view. To the extent you recognize that you're wrong, admit it and apologize. If you don't feel you're in the wrong:

   a. Provide relevant details in a non-defensive manner

      "Here's how I see the situation."

      "There are some things I'd like to share with you."

      "I'd like to give you my perspective."

      "I have some information you might not be aware of."

   b. Ask for feedback

      "What thoughts do you have about what I said?"

      "Did my explanation clarify the situation?"

      "Do you need any more information?"

3. Identify the consequences of the conflict, past, present and, if not resolved, future (this provides additional rationale for resolving the conflict).

4. Seek a solution that works for both (all) of you.

   a. Discuss possible solutions.

   b. Evaluate alternative solutions and agree on the one most consistent with the associated value(s).

   c. Decide on a plan of action for implementing the solution. *Who* will do *what* and by *when*?

   d. Agree on a follow-up to evaluate the plan of action.

When you have an issue with someone

1. Decide if the issue is worth pursuing. It's important to confront others when their behavior is:

   a. Damaging your relationship

   b. Hurting others

   c. Hurting the offender

2. Prepare ahead of time.

   a. Choose the right time and place.

   b. Believe the best about people.

   c. Talk in person whenever possible.

   d. Plan what you will say. Think about what you'd say if someone came to you for advice about a similar situation (This will help you be more objective).

3. Give relevant information.

   a. Communicate in a courteous manner.

   b. Be descriptive rather than evaluative.

c.   Focus on what the person actually said or did ("You criticized me in front of my staff"), not intentions ("You deliberately tried to make me look bad"). It's difficult to prove another person's intentions, and inferences about why they said or did something will usually put them on the defensive.

d.   Use "I" messages.

e.   Ask for feedback.

4.   Listen and show understanding by reflecting both content and feeling.

5.   Seek solutions.

a.   Ask for suggestions.

b.   Offer suggestions.

6.   Evaluate alternatives and reach agreement.

a.   Material issues should be dealt with by negotiating a mutually satisfactory (win-win) agreement.

b.   Find a solution that maintains or enhances the relationship.

VALUE-DRIVEN STRATEGIC PLANNING EXERCISE

PURPOSE: To facilitate values-driven strategic planning with individuals, teams, or organizations.

Background

Values pertain to ends and to means for accomplishing these ends. Thus, values guide all the key components in the planning process and allow a consistent and integrated approach to management. Organizational values guide decisions about mission, vision, culture, strategy, and action. Of course, you must be alert to the complexity and changing dynamics of the market and other elements in the situation within which you are functioning. In other words, think strategically. Something is strategic if it:

- Establishes direction
- Impacts organizational values
- Has organization-wide implications
- Impacts the future
- Affects competitive position
- Has a long-term perspective
- Involves calculated risks
- Guides action

In the past, it was possible to map out relatively firm 5-year strategic plans, but in the networked economy that is no longer realistic. Situational changes may require changes in goals, objectives, and/or plans. Because of this, clarity about mission, vision, and values takes on added significance. And clarity about values is important because values are fundamental.

Instructions

This exercise provides a worksheet for consolidating information about the key elements involved in formulating strategy. It can be used by an individual for personal planning or by a group to facilitate team or organizational planning. In actual practice, the responses for mission, vision, and values may each be recorded on one or two sheets of paper (easel paper for a team or an organization). Then a separate set of sheets can be prepared for each combination of goal, the objectives related to the goal, and action steps.

When used as a large group intervention, the worksheet allows the entire system to operate "on the same page." Once the process is complete, relevant information for individuals, teams, and the overall organization can be placed on a computer to facilitate communication, revision, and accountability.

Values-Driven Planning Worksheet

Focus of Attention: ☐ Myself   ☐ The team   ☐ The organization

Mission (Purpose, reason for existing)

Vision (Dreams for the future)

Values (Standards of importance for moving toward vision)

(Note: For examples of specific statements of mission, vision, and values, see *The Mission Statement Book: 301 Corporate Mission Statements from America's Top Companies*, by Jeffrey Abrams, 1999.)

Goals, objectives, and action plans:

* Goals (general directions for moving toward vision)
* Objectives (specific results for each goal by a specific time)
* Action Plans (sequence of actions that will accomplish each objective, which generally include "who," "what action," and "when")

(Note: Add additional goals, objectives, and action plans as needed)

Goal #1:

Objective:

Action Plans:

Objective:

Action Plans:

Goal #2:

Objective:

Action Plans:

Objective:

Action Plans:

Goal #3:

Objective:

Action Plans:

Objective:

Action Plans:

PART 4

VALUES-DRIVEN MULTI-LEVEL CHANGE

7. **Building a Values-Driven Culture**

   To define a values-driven culture, offer a set of criteria for evaluating organizational values, and provide guidelines, instruments, and exercises for building a culture defined by values. Includes the Values Assessment Inventory™, and the Values Identification Survey.

8. **Removing Barriers to Organizational Effectiveness**

   Describe a systems approach to motivation that can be used with individuals, teams, and organizations to assess their current situation and make change decisions. Describes Motivational System Mapping™, a structured facilitation process.

7

BUILDING A VALUES-DRIVEN CULTURE

PURPOSE: To define a values-driven culture, offer a set of criteria for evaluating organizational values, and provide guidelines, instruments, and exercises for building a culture defined by values.

What Is a Values-Driven Culture?

Do these comments sound familiar:

- "We already have a values-based organization."
- "We did the values thing last year; now we're working on strategic planning."
- "We don't have time to think about values; if we're going to stay competitive, we need to focus on results."
- "Values may help our image, but what do they have to do with performance?"

Organizational leaders and managers who make statements like these often lack understanding of the role played by values in either fostering or inhibiting performance, and what it takes to establish and maintain a results-oriented, values-driven culture.

For our purposes, a culture can be considered values-driven if a systematic effort has been made to:

1. Select organizational values according to objective criteria,
2. Define the values behaviorally,
3. Embed the values in key management systems, such as employee selection, day-to-day supervision, and performance evaluation, and
4. Remains committed to the values when under pressure.

This chapter offers a set of criteria for selecting values, and provides guidelines and tools for defining values behaviorally, and embedding them in culture for long-term success.

Criteria for Selecting Values

Historically, OD practitioners have been the champions of healthy work values, serving the mutual interests of human beings and organizations (see, for example, Bennis, 1969; Tannenbaum & Davis, 1969; Burke,

1982, 1997). Today, however, we are under intense pressure to help organizations increase productivity, efficiency, and short-term profits at all costs with little regard for other values. The risk is that we will become co-opted, tearing down the values that the profession has emphasized in the past. Is it possible to help today's fast-paced, technology-driven organizations achieve their goals, while continuing to advocate the humanistic, democratic, and developmental values upon which the field was founded? This is possible if we can articulate objective criteria that align the energies of individuals, teams, and organizations.

Putting values under a microscope conjures up images of scrutinizing motherhood, the flag, and apple pie. Many people become defensive when their values are questioned, regarding this as a personal affront. They expect you to show respect for their values simply because they embrace them, and are easily offended if you don't. People develop a vested interest in their values, sometimes to the point of fanatical allegiance. When listening to them, it often becomes clear they believe their values are the right ones, the best ones, the only ones.

Scrutinizing values is necessary, however, because they have either a positive or negative impact on decisions, priorities, strategies, plans, and behavior—there's no such thing as a value with a neutral impact. Throughout history, values have been used to justify everything from the noble to the heinous. Each day we read about atrocities being committed in the name of national security, religious freedom, patriotism, ethnic or racial pride, and other values. Similarly, organizations justify downsizing, restructuring, plant closings, mergers, acquisitions, and hostile takeovers in the name of corporate survival, profitability, efficiency, and shareholder value. We can engage in endless debate about whether these are the best or even the real values, only to remain adrift in a sea of subjectivity. The need to assess values has become imperative, because globalization has made organizations such powerful institutions and their decisions affect us all.

Previously (see Hultman, 2002) I suggested four criteria for assessing the effectiveness of values: viability, balance, alignment, and authenticity. I define *effective* as the ability to get desired results. The criteria, which themselves are values, should be viewed as a source of hypotheses open for discussion, debate, and research. Table 7.1 summarizes the four criteria and the related issues for each one; these terms will be defined in the sections below. The Values Assessment Inventory ™ (VAI) at the end of this chapter allows you to assess values according to the four criteria.

Table 7.1
Criteria and Related Issues

Criteria	Issues
Viability	• Value content • Value functions
Balance	• Balanced value representation • Balanced value emphasis
Alignment	• Intrapersonal conflict • Interpersonal conflict • Discrepancies between espoused and actual values
Authenticity	• Offering real reasons for actions

Viability

Viability can be defined as the degree to which values are workable in the current business climate. Viability centers on the content and functions of values.

Value Content

As mentioned at the beginning, some organizations boast about being "values-based," but all organizations are values-based in the sense that all decisions are guided by values. The more important questions have to do with the particular values that are chosen, and how those values guide action. These questions are crucial, because not all values are created equal. Research has shown consistently that high-performing organizations have values that differ from others, whether performance is measured by financial criteria, such as stock returns or revenue growth, or by corporate longevity or sustainability. Results from several recent studies are summarized in Table 7.2.

These findings reveal a great deal of overlap. In the area of personal competence, the emphasis is on *excellence* and *learning*, i.e. using and further developing one's knowledge and skills. Such values allow organizations to do quality work in the present, be creative, and adapt to changing conditions. In the area of social competence, the emphasis is on *empowerment* and *ownership*. It would be difficult to overstate the relevance of these values to performance. Kotter & Heskett (1992) found that revenues for firms with values affirming the legitimate interests of employees, customers, and stockholders (ownership), and encouraging leadership at all organizational levels (empowerment), increased by an average of 682% over an 11 year period, as compared to 166% for firms that didn't have those. Employees are more productive and satisfied when opportunities exist for them to act like stakeholders.

In the area of personal integrity, values pertaining to *honesty* and *fairness* are mentioned in every study. Kouzes & Posner (1995) found that honesty was ranked first among characteristics of admired leaders, followed by forward-looking (setting a vision), and inspiring (motivating people to follow the vision). Unless leaders are honest, nobody cares about their vision. In the area of social integrity, the focus is on establishing a *community*. De Geus (1997) found that longevity doesn't depend on the ability of a company to return investment to shareholders: profitability was a *symptom* of corporate health, but not a *predictor* or *determinant* of it. In long-lived companies, ROI was a means to the end of creating and maintaining a community. In these companies optimizing capital was secondary to optimizing people.

Consistent with De Geus' findings, Collins & Porras (1994) reported that the key difference between visionary and comparison companies was that the former possessed a rock-solid core ideology that didn't change over time. They concluded that superior market performance was not a function of having profit as a primary value. However, some managers are likely to view this counter-intuitive finding with skepticism. Logic tells them that organizations can't be "humanistic" and "practical" at the same time, but the research clearly indicates that this is not only possible but also necessary. The challenge for leaders is to consider the needs of both organizations and people, i.e. to be practical and humanistic.

Table 7.2
The Impact of Values on Performance

Source	Values		
Collins & Porras (1994). *Build to Last: Successful Habits of Visionary Companies.* A study of the values of 18 visionary companies.	**Personal Competence** Product/service excellence Continuous improvement/learning Creativity/innovation	**Social Competence** Empowerment Contribution to society Customer service Profit	
	Personal Character Honesty/integrity	**Social Character** Respect & concern for employees	
Jac Fitz-Enz (1997). *The 8 Practices of Exceptional Companies.* A study of the values of the top 5% of 1000 companies studied over a four-year period, using a rigorous set of quantitative and financial performance criteria.	**Personal Competence** Innovation and risk Continuous improvement	**Social Competence** Balance of human and financial values Commitment to a long-term core strategy Linking culture and systems	
	Personal Character (Honesty is implied)	**Social Character** Extensive two-way communication Partnering with stakeholders Collaboration	
Arie De Geus (1997). *The Living Company: Habits for Survival in a Turbulent Business Environment.* A study of 27 companies older and larger than Royal Dutch/Shell, founded in 1907.	**Personal Competence** Anticipating the need to adapt and change Developing individual and organizational potential Learning Productivity	**Social Competence** Conservative financing Corporate survival (long-term interests) Empowerment Tolerance (openness to ideas) On-going assessment of internal structures	
	Personal Character Fairness Honesty	**Social Character** Cohesion (Belonging) Communication Creating and maintaining a community Networking Trust	

Source	Values	
Kouzes & Posner (1995). *The Leadership Challenge: How to Keep Getting Extraordinary Things Done in Organizations.* Most admired leader characteristic (values) in rank order, from surveys of 20,000 people on four continents.	**Personal Competence** 4. Competent 7. Broad-minded 8. Intelligent 10. Dependable 13. Imaginative 15. Determined 16. Mature 17. Ambitious 20. Independent **Personal Character** 1. Honest 5. Fair-minded 9. Straightforward 11. Courageous 19. Self-controlled	**Social Competence** 2. Forward-looking 3. Inspiring **Social Character** 6. Supportive 12. Cooperative 14. Caring 18. Loyal

One more point needs to be made about the content of values: values aren't defined by what we say, but by what we do. To be considered viable, therefore, these behaviors must produce effective outcomes. When an organization establishes or changes its values, it's very important to give those values clear behavioral definitions, so employees will know what's expected of them. I try to discover what a value means in an organization by asking questions like this: "You say that teamwork is important here. What behaviors can I expect to see reflecting that value?" In addition, research provided some excellent guidelines for defining values behaviorally. As reported by Buckingham & Coffman (1999), for example, in a twenty-five year study of over a million employees, the Gallup Organization found that the following 10 management practices were associated with productivity, profitability, employee retention, and customer satisfaction:

1. Clarifying performance expectations.
2. Providing necessary materials and equipment.
3. Provide opportunities for employees to do what they do best.
4. Give employees recognition for good work at least once a week.
5. Care about employees as persons.
6. Encourages employee development.
7. Consider employee's opinions.
8. Make employee's feel their job is important.

9. Talk to employees about progress.
10. Provided opportunities for employees to learn and grow.

In this study, the other factors associated with the four business outcomes were: having co-workers committed to doing quality work, and having a best friend at work. As shown is Table 7.3, these 12 factors can help define the research-validated values.

Table 7.3
Relationship between Values and Organizational Practices

	Personal	Social
Competence	**Excellence** • Clarifying performance expectations • Providing necessary materials and equipment • Provide opportunities for employees to do what they do best • Give employees recognition for good work at least once a week • Having co-workers committed to doing quality work **Learning** • Encourages employee development • Talk to employees about progress • Provided opportunities for employees to learn and grow	**Empowerment** • Consider employee's opinions • Make employee's feel their job is important
Character	**Honesty and Fairness** These values are implied	**Community** • Have a best friend at work • Care about employees as persons

Most of the practices identified in this research have to do with the relationship between managers and employees; organizations that hire and develop managers who use these practices get better results than those that don't.

Value Functions

Values not only vary by content, but also by function or purpose. Recall that a distinction can be made between terminal and instrumental values. Terminal values define the overall goal we want to achieve and have two components: our purpose or personal mission defines *why* we exist, and our dreams for the future or personal vision defines *what* we want to become. Instrumental values are preferred modes of conduct, defining *how* we plan to fulfill our purpose and dreams. These values focus on *competence*, which focuses on abilities, and integrity, which focuses on *character*. We're not only industrious problem-solvers but also ethical and moral beings, concerned with questions about good and bad, right and wrong. Competence and character have both a personal and social dimension, allowing us to distinguish four sub-needs:

- **Personal competence**: People need to view themselves and be viewed by others as being skilled, knowledgeable, and capable.

- **Social competence**: People need to view themselves and be viewed by others as making a difference.

- **Personal** character: People need to view themselves and be viewed by others as being ethical and moral; this is a requirement for self-respect.

- **Social character**: People need to be accepted by others.

The function of values is to meet these various personal and social needs. Table 7.4 provides some common instrumental values in today's world, categorized by sub-needs. This list isn't meant to be exhaustive, and it's open for debate where a particular value should be placed, but this does show the usefulness of the four-fold model.

Any particular value can function to meet our needs by either:

- Defending against perceived threat (Defensive Value)

- Maintaining the status quo (Stabilizing Value)

- Fostering forward movement (Growth Value)

These distinctions were inspired by the work of Maslow (1968), who divided values into three functional categories: growth values, healthy-regression ("coasting" values), and defensive-values (unhealthy regression). He maintained that people have an intrinsic motivation for growth, but they need homeostatic values for peace, rest, and relaxation. He asserted that more mature and healthy people place greater emphasis on growth values, but that "coasting" values are always necessary. He also maintained that defensive-values, which protect against pain, fear, loss and threat, are a *sine qua non* precondition for growth, but cautioned that they can also inhibit growth. Values for conformity and routine, for example, can undermine creativity and innovation.

The instrumental values in Table 7.4 are classified as defensive, stabilizing, and growth in Tables 7.5, 7.6, and 7.7.

Table 7.4
Instrumental Values Matrix

	PERSONAL		SOCIAL	
COMPETENCE	Accomplishment	Logical	Adding value	Participation
	Achievement	Mastery	Affirmation	Peace
	Adaptability	Material possessions	A sense of community	Philanthropy
	Advancement	Merit	Authority	Power
	Adventurous	Opportunity	Balance home/work	Prestige
	Ambition	Optimism	Boundaryless	Profitability
	Caution	Originality	Community involvement	Progress
	Comfort	Productivity	Competition	Recognition
	Creativity	Professionalism	Contribution	Self-interest
	Credentials	Quality	Control	Service
	Delight	Responsibility	Customer satisfaction	Social awareness
	Developing one's potential	Responsiveness	Developing others	Status
	Effectiveness	Results	Empowerment	Stewardship
	Efficiency	Risk-taking	Environmentalism	Synergism
	Enthusiasm	Routine	Financial growth	Territory
	Excellence	Security	Generosity	Tradition
	Flexibility	Self-starter	Giving something back	
	Freedom	Seniority	Glory	
	Growth	Speed	Good will	
	Humor/fun	Spontaneity	Harmony	
	Imagination	Stability	Honor	
	Improvement	Status quo	Humanitarianism	
	Independence	Strategic focus	Influence	
	Initiative	Stretch goals	Involvement	
	Innovation	Success	Making a difference	
	Individuality	Timeliness	Mentoring	
	Intelligence	Variety	Mutual interest	
	Intuition	Winning	Order	
	Knowledge	Wisdom	Organizational growth	
	Learning		Ownership	
CHARACTER	Accountability	Morality	Accepting others	Friendship
	Authenticity	Obedience	Alignment	Helpfulness
	Commitment	Perseverance	Approval	Inclusiveness
	Congruence	Reliability	Assertiveness	Interdependence
	Consistency	Self-control	Belonging	Justice
	Courage	Self-respect	Candor	Kindness
	Credibility	Sincerity	Caring	Love
	Dedication	Situational ethics	Cohesiveness	Loyalty
	Deference	Spirituality	Collaboration	Mercy
	Dependability	Truth	Companionship	Networking
	Dignity	Willpower	Compassion	Openness
	Diligence		Confidentiality	Partnering
	Discipline		Cooperation	Patience
	Discretion		Coordination	Politeness
	Ethics		Courtesy	Popularity
	Expediency		Diplomacy	Relationships
	Faith		Diversity	Respect
	Genuineness		Equality	Tact
	Honesty		Fairness	Teamwork
	Humility		Faithfulness	Tolerance
	Integrity		Fellowship	Trust
	Law abiding		Forgiveness	

Table 7.5
Defensive Values

	PERSONAL		SOCIAL	
COMPETENCE	Caution Clean Independence Material possessions Security Speed	Winning	Competition Control Glory Honor Order Power	Prestige Recognition Self-interest Status Seniority Territory
CHARACTER	Deference Expediency Obedience Situational ethics		Approval Courtesy Diplomacy Loyalty	Politeness Popularity Tact

Table 7.6
Stabilizing Values

	PERSONAL		SOCIAL	
COMPETENCE	Comfort Credentials Dependability Efficiency Productivity	Professionalism Reliability Routine Self-discipline Stability	Authority Balance home/work Harmony Order Peace	Status quo Tradition
CHARACTER	Consistency Dedication Dignity Diligence Discretion Ethics Honesty Humility Integrity Law abiding Morality	Self-control Self-respect Sincerity	Accountability Belonging Candor Caring Companionship Compassion Confidentiality Coordination Fairness Faithfulness Fellowship	Forgiveness Friendship Justice Kindness Love Mercy Patience Respect Tact Tolerance Trust

Table 7.7
Growth Values

	PERSONAL		SOCIAL	
COMPETENCE	Adaptability	Learning	Adding value	Mutual interests
	Adventurous	Logical	Affirmation	Organizational growth
	Congruence	Mastery	A sense of community	Ownership
	Creativity	Merit	Boundaryless	Participation
	Curiosity	Opportunity	Community involvement	Philanthropy
	Delight	Optimism	Contribution	Profitability
	Effectiveness	Originality	Customer satisfaction	Progress
	Enthusiasm	Perseverance	Developing others	Service
	Excellence	Quality	Empowerment	Social awareness
	Flexibility	Responsibility	Environmentalism	Stewardship
	Freedom	Responsiveness	Financial growth	Synergism
	Growth	Results	Generosity	Volunteerism
	Humor/fun	Risk-taking	Giving something back	
	Imagination	Self-starter	Good will	
	Improvement	Spontaneity	Humanitarianism	
	Initiative	Strategic focus	Human rights	
	Innovation	Stretch goals	Influence	
	Intelligence	Timeliness	Involvement	
	Intuition	Variety	Making a difference	
	Knowledge		Mentoring	
CHARACTER	Authenticity		Accepting others	Inclusiveness
	Commitment		Alignment	Interdependence
	Courage		Cohesiveness	Networking
	Credibility		Collaboration	Openness
	Faith		Cooperation	Partnering
	Genuineness		Diversity	Relationships
	Truth		Equality	Teamwork
			Helpfulness	

Examining the value system of an individual, team, or organization will reveal a combination of defensive, stabilizing and growth values. In fact, as shown in Figure 7.1, value systems can be classified as predominately D, S, or G. No matter how hard you try, it's unrealistic to think that D or S values can or should be eliminated entirely. For example, safety (a D value) is a core value at NASA and in other organizations where there are large risks. Also, honesty (an S value) is a necessary condition for healthy and effective relationships in any team and organization. Nevertheless, most of the values listed in Table 7.2 are growth values; this is where organizations need to place their emphasis if they plan to remain competitive in the new economy.

Figure 7.1

Value Mix In Defensive, Stabilizing, and Growth Organizations

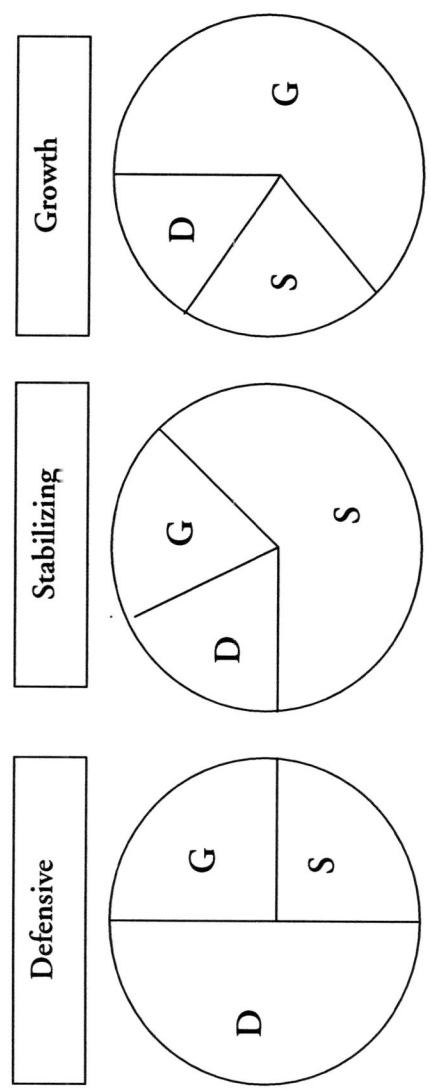

In my view, the best way to revitalize organizations is to decrease conditions associated with D values and increase conditions favorable to G values—eliminating threats and adding opportunities. When I work with teams or organizations on values issues, I often ask people to estimate the amount of emphasis given to D, S, and G values, and then to generate ideas for decreasing D values and increasing G values. This often deepens people's understanding of organizational issues, and generates useful suggestions for dealing with those issues. Recently I posed this question to a group of internal consultants at a Fortune 100 aerospace company. Six subgroups working independently were remarkably consistent in estimating the company's values to be about 60% D, 30% S, and 20% G. The organization was losing market share to a competitor and needed a culture change to be revitalized. These internal consultants agreed that the percentages for D and G values needed to be reversed; their challenge was to figure out how this could be done proactively, to avert a potential financial disaster. Table 7.8 provides a checklist of questions that can help determine the viability of a value. The Values Identification Survey (VIS) at the end of the chapter allows you to assess the content and function of values for individuals, teams, and organizations.

Balance

Balance can be defined as the degree to which values are given proper emphasis relative to one another. There are two chief types of balance: balanced representation and balanced emphasis.

Balanced Value Representation

Elsewhere (Hultman, 2002) I've argued that a balanced value system *must* contain values relating to the four categories of personal and social needs: mastery (personal competence), a sense of contribution (social competence), self-respect (personal character), and acceptance (social character). This ensures that the important areas of human functioning are covered and provides for accountability. Imagine what it would be like if an organization lacked standards of importance for individual performance (personal competence), or if no effort were made to show employees how their efforts contribute to the whole (social competence). Similarly, imagine if an organization asked employees to compromise their ethical standards (personal character), or if people felt marginalized by their color, age, sex, or ethnicity (social character). It doesn't take long to realize that all four types of values are necessary for effective functioning.

Table 7.8
Viable Value Checklist

- Is it favorable to growth?
- Does it contribute to a sense of wholeness and completeness?
- Does it encourage people to achieve their potential?
- Does it foster a positive sense of self-esteem?
- Does it free people to pursue their aspirations?
- Does it take a long-range perspective?
- Is it based on accurate beliefs?
- Is it based on trust?
- Is it in tune with current business realities?
- Is it defined clearly?
- Are the behaviors chosen to pursue it effective?
- Does it produce the desired results?
- Are potential consequences taken into consideration?
- Does it have the intended impact?
- Does it satisfy people's needs and wants?

I've worked with organizations that lacked values in one or more key areas, resulting in a variety of problems. For example, one organization had three stated values: excellence (personal competence), customer success (social competence), and teamwork (social character). They didn't have any stated values in the area of personal character, however, which resulted in questionable business practices and customer complaints. Another organization had five values: trying your best (personal competence), developing your potential (personal competence), delighting the customer (social competence), contributing to society (social competence) and being honest (personal character). They didn't have any values in the area of social character, however, and this surfaced as petty bickering and internal competition.

In contrast, at a health-care organization where I facilitated the establishment of organizational values, the values chosen were excellence (personal competence), service and stewardship (social competence), integrity (personal character), and teamwork (social character). At another health-care organization, the values selected were creativity and efficiency (personal competence), enthusiasm (social competence), honesty (personal character), and compassion (social character). Having all four categories represented allowed these organizations to balance their business and people interests.

Balanced Value Emphasis

Balanced emphasis or priority must be given to the values chosen to meet the four psychological and social needs. Such balance is often difficult to achieve, however, because a value system is hierarchical. This doesn't mean that the order remains constant; values shift in emphasis depending on the situation, such as when people go home after work. Nevertheless, every organization has a value that's at the top of the pecking order—it operates like a CEO—and this value has an overarching influence on other values in the system. For example, I once worked at a mental health clinic where the top three values were (1) the number of clients, (2) completing client paperwork, and (3) quality of treatment (Note: these weren't the stated values, but rather my assessment as a member of the culture). When push came to shove, numbers and paperwork invariably took precedence over quality of service.

At a large manufacturing company where I once served as a consultant, the top value was "products shipped." This value was given so much emphasis that employees shipped unfinished or broken products just to meet their daily quota, fully aware that customers would return them. I've worked with other organizations that placed such a high emphasis on performance (personal competence) that teams failed to develop cohesiveness (social character), and others that emphasized speed at the expense of quality (both personal competence values). It doesn't take long to figure out what's most important in an organization; as you listen to people talk and watch them in action, the real priorities become abundantly clear.

Finding the right balance among values is an on-going challenge, requiring organizations to monitor continuously the potential impact of decisions on the integrity of their value system. This is another area where OD practitioners can make an important contribution. Table 7.9 summarizes some consequences of overemphasizing and underemphasizing values, along with suggestions for improving balance. You can easily add your own examples to the model.

Alignment

Alignment can be defined as "being in line" or "coordinated;" that is, values are aligned based on the degree to which they are compatible. We will focus on three types of alignment, *intrapersonal, interpersonal*, and *organizational*. Intrapersonal alignment, or what many people refer to as "congruence," is compatibility among an individual's values; interpersonal alignment refers to compatibility between the values of two or more individuals; organizational alignment refers to compatibility between personal and organizational values. In all three cases, alignment also refers to consistency between espoused and actual values.

The opposite of alignment is misalignment, i.e. lacking compatibility. Both imbalance and misalignment cause conflict, but for different reasons. With imbalance, the conflict stems from either overemphasizing or underemphasizing values; with incongruence, the conflict stems from a basic incompatibility between values—like mixing oil and water. Let's talk about intrapersonal, interpersonal, and organizational value conflict in more detail.

Table 7.9
Consequences of Lack of Balance and Ways to Achieve Balance

Value	Overemphasis	Underemphasis	Ways to Achieve Balance
Mastery (Personal Competence)	Fear of failure Unrealistic goals, deadlines Insecurity Stress, frustration Anger, resentment Feeling used Feel treated as a number Internal competition Exploitation Emphasis on tasks at the expense of relationships Unionization, strikes Sabotage, rebellion	Poor quality Inefficiency Customer complaints Lack of performance goals Carelessness, mistakes Loss of business Waste of talent, ability Underutilizing people Tension between productive and unproductive employees	Set performance goals that are meaningful, achievable, measurable, and controllable Emphasize developing one's potential Focus on learning, instead of labeling performance in terms of success or failure Strive for excellence Balance work/home life Think creatively
A Sense of Contribution (Social Competence)	Fear of insignificance Making arbitrary distinctions between the importance of jobs Status issues Emphasis on "hype"	Lack of fulfillment Indifference, complacency View job as just a paycheck Lack of recognition Lack of commitment Lack of ownership Cynicism	Praise good performance Point out how a person's work contributes to the whole Stress mutual interests Strive to add value Give credit where credit's due Avoid minimizing contributions Emphasize customer success Focus on stewardship
Self-Respect (Personal Character)	Fear of being judged Emphasis on formality Lack of spontaneity Fear of offending people	Hostile work environment Harassment Insensitivity Lack of accountability Labeling people Lack of trust	Clarify acceptable and unacceptable behaviors Hold people accountable Follow the "Golden Rule" Do the right thing, even if it's unpopular Present yourself as someone worthy of trust Deal with issues directly Maintain a commitment to the truth Honor commitments

Value	Overemphasis	Underemphasis	Ways to Achieve Balance
	Fear of rejection	Prejudice, discrimination	Invite participation and involvement
	Social club atmosphere	Alienation	Stress team success
	Emphasis on relationships at the expense of tasks	Cliques, in-groups, out-groups	Champion inclusiveness and diversity
	Deadlines are missed	Favoritism	Avoid unhealthy competition
Acceptance (Social Character)	Compromising honesty to maintain acceptance	Lack of cohesiveness	Strive for cohesiveness and cooperation
	Pressure to conform	Lack of cooperation	Foster open communication
	Office politics	Lack of teamwork	Eliminate discrimination
		Communication problems	Challenge stereotypes
		Lack of diversity, inclusiveness	
		Lack of participation involvement	
		Lack of trust	

Intrapersonal Conflict

Recall that values serve to maintain and enhance a person's self-worth. One's sense of self-worth can be placed on a continuum extending from completely conditional at one end to completely unconditional at the other. Although some people lean toward the conditional and others lean toward the unconditional, most of us hold a mixture of beliefs representing both types. One's sense of self-worth tends to ebb and flow during the course of daily life. We notice, for example, how a person's self-confidence rises and falls with their performance. Moving from conditional to unconditional self-worth is a growth process that unfolds over time.

People who have a mixture of conditional and unconditional self-conceptions often struggle with internal conflict. If the conditional beliefs prevail, they tend to settle for defensive or stabilizing values; if more unconditional beliefs prevail, they are freer to embrace growth values.

Sometimes people have trouble identifying sources of internal conflicts, and coaching or counseling is needed to uncover and resolve them. One time, for example, a supervisor who was terminated for failure to meet project deadlines came to me for help. He revealed that as a child he was taught to present a can-do attitude to others. His self-worth was based on being positive and optimistic. Whenever his manager asked if a project was on schedule, therefore, he always said yes, even if there was no way it could be completed on time. Through coaching he realized that his need to be optimistic prevented him from being honest with himself or others. Separating his self-worth from being optimistic freed him to make more realistic work assessments.

Intrapersonal conflicts may also stem from competing values within a person's value system. Rokeach (1973) explained that a person could have conflict between two character values (honesty and sensitivity), between two competence values (logical and creative), or between character and competence value (humility and ambition). Such conflicts need to be identified and resolved, so they don't undermine a person's effectiveness.

Also every choice involves tradeoffs, because making one choice means eliminating or deemphasizing others. Parenting, for example, involves a trade off of personal freedom to raise a family. If people are prepared to make the tradeoffs associated with a choice, they can still remain congruent. If they're not prepared, however, they'll feel trapped by the choice and seek a way of escape. It's crucial, therefore, to identify tradeoffs associated with choices and determine whether or not they're acceptable.

Interpersonal Conflict

Value conflict between two or more people typically manifests itself as disagreements about goals, priorities, methods, and beliefs, resulting in power struggles, hidden agendas, manipulation, internal competition, and mistrust. In addition, when people with different levels of self-worth are required to work together, this often leads to interpersonal conflict. Those with a higher sense of self-worth move toward defensive or stabilizing values; those with a lower sense of self-worth move toward growth values. Resolving such conflicts involves helping people identify and work through underlying value issues (see Steps for Resolving Conflict).

Organizational Conflict

This kind of conflict can be understood as lack of alignment or a poor fit between personal, team, and/or organizational values. The concept of alignment is controversial. Some people view this as manipulating employees to achieve organizational ends. However, attempts to force alignment never work for long; they only serve to increase conflict and mistrust. They drive values issues underground, resurfacing as passive-aggressive behavior, open defiance, sabotage, morale problems, and turnover.

There's nothing wrong with seeking alignment per se. Increasing consistency between personal and organizational values results in higher levels of morale and productivity. For example, a Gallup Poll found that organizations had higher profits when workers believed (1) they have a chance to do what they do best each day, (2) their opinions mattered, (3) their fellow workers cared about quality, and (4) a connection existed between their work and the company's mission (Grant, 1998). In addition, numerous studies examining employee perception of value congruence with the organization found that this has a desirable effect on such outcomes as job satisfaction, commitment, involvement, intentions to leave, and turnover (see, for example, Cable & Judge, 1996; Harris & Mossholder, 1996; Choa, et al, 1994; Chatman 1991; O'Reilly, Chatman, & Caldwell, 1991; Lee & Mowday, 1987). Thus, employees perform better and are more satisfied with their work when organizational values are aligned with their personal values.

The issue isn't whether or not to work toward alignment, but how. I believe the best way is to create a *shared* purpose and vision where people can freely align themselves based on their personal purposes and visions. Alignment based on value integration is an on-going process. Rokeach (1973) estimated that people have between 30-40 values in their value system. A team or organization would reflect a much larger number. Like personal alignment, therefore, it's unrealistic to think that a team or organization could achieve complete integration. Also, people can agree on values but disagree on their priority. For these reasons, alignment is better seen as a dynamic process. I've consulted in situations where there was alignment at the team level, but disconnects between team, departmental, and overall organizational values. Increasing integration among these levels requires an atmosphere where people can discuss their differences openly, identify tradeoffs involved with decisions, and manage them effectively. People are more willing to support decisions they don't agree with if they've been given an opportunity for input, and they trust that their input will be considered. This is especially true if they trust that the consideration seeks a win-win resolution of the conflict when possible.

Bringing about alignment is a continuous process, and it's one of the most important strategic functions of leadership. To accomplish this, leaders must be willing to engage in on-going dialogue with employees about what's important to them, explain what's important to the organization, and work to bring about balance between the two. Such alignment is particularly important because it focuses individual energy in a common direction, and creates synergy that cannot exist without it. Actually alignment isn't as daunting as it sounds. Employees may use a wide variety of terms to describe what's important to them, but most of their input will fall into the four-fold model: personal and social competence, and personal and social character. Employees want opportunities to use their skills, learn, and make a contribution, within an atmosphere of mutual respect and belonging. Organizations need a capable and adaptable workforce, workers who act like owners, owners who care about workers, honesty and fairness, and a community with a shared identity. There's much common ground here. OD can make a significant impact by helping organizations find and maintain such common ground.

Discrepancies between Espoused and Actual Values

Misalignment between espoused and actual values can accompany intrapersonal, interpersonal, and organizational conflicts. As mentioned earlier, regardless of what values people espouse, others will infer their real values from what they do. The actual values of a team or organization are revealed by what it rewards and punishes—this reveals its true standards of importance. Schein (1992) said that leaders can quickly convey their own priorities, values, and assumptions by consistently linking rewards and punishments to behavioral expectations. Leaders who fail to do this create confusion. I remember standing next to an employee once that pointed to a list of the organization's noble-sounding values, and said cynically, "All they really care about is getting us to do the most work for the least amount of pay."

Sometimes discrepancies between espoused and actual values represent hypocrisy—not "walking the talk"—while at other times they represent a lack of skill or emotional intelligence. In the former case, people should be held accountable for choosing behavior consistent with the values; in the latter case, training and/or coaching is indicated.

Inconsistencies between two behaviors—such as being supportive on one occasion and critical on another—could reflect a value conflict or other issues. More information is usually necessary to identify reasons for such inconsistencies. Finally, differences between actual and desired values pose no problem, as long as people are actively working toward the latter. In this situation, people will grant the organization a "grace period." Values are ideals; people can accept inconsistency as long as progress is made toward those ideals.

Even well conceived values won't have a positive impact on performance, however, unless those values are embedded in key management systems, such as the selection system and the performance management process (i.e. setting performance goals and learning objectives, and conducting performance evaluation discussions). A value system isn't complete unless every performance competency can be classified under a specific value; this is one of the most effective ways to operationally define the values. Consistent with this, Collins & Porras (1994) found that visionary companies:

- More thoroughly orient employees to their values,
- More carefully select and nurture senior management based on a fit with the values, and
- Attain more consistent alignment with the values, in such aspects as purpose, vision, goals, strategy, tactics, culture, and organizational design.

To facilitate the embedding of values, guidelines for values-driven decision-making, problem-solving, conflict resolution, and strategic planning are included in the Supplemental Guidelines section at the end of the chapter.

Authenticity

I define authenticity as the degree to which values are expressed—verbally and behaviorally—in a genuine, sincere manner. The authenticity of an organization's values and alignment with the values are more important than the content of the values (Collins and Porras, 1994). Content does matter, as the research described above indicates, but only if the values are authentic.

Earlier I indicated that people's core need is to have a sense of self-worth. We're not only motivated to enhance our self-worth, but also to protect it from perceived threat. Here's where authenticity comes into play. Authenticity is offering the *real* reasons for our actions, while lack of authenticity is giving plausible but false reasons for what we do ("I did it out of fairness"). Authenticity is similar to Senge's (1990) concept of a commitment to the truth, which he identifies as a criterion for the discipline of personal mastery. It's also related to what McAniff (1999) calls level four truth—where rational and emotional intelligence combine. Inauthentic values manifest themselves as defensive behavior, which leads to interpersonal conflict, mistrust and, ultimately, blocks alignment toward vision.

A relationship exists between authenticity and self-justification. People use both authentic and rationalized self-justification. Asking people *why* they did something can be perceived as a threat to their self-worth, so they must decide whether to be candid or to rationalize. All defense mechanisms serve the purpose of helping people maintain a sense of self-worth. Rationalization is the defense mechanism most closely tied to values, however, because values are the justifications we offer for decisions and actions.

People often rationalize when confronted with discrepancies between espoused and actual values. There is, however, a difference between intrapersonal misalignment (incongruence) and rationalizing. With intrapersonal misalignment, a conflict exists among values (cooperation and competition) or between values and behavior (honesty and telling "white lies"); with rationalization, a false value underlies the reasons offered, while the real value—maintaining self-worth—remains hidden. No one says, "I'm doing this to salvage my self-image," but this is the underlying motive behind many actions in the workplace. Defending self-worth is so basic that even very self-aware and confident people are capable of doing it unconsciously. The degree of defensiveness varies greatly among people, of course, but increasing self-awareness offers more freedom to pursue growth values.

Fostering greater authenticity in a team or organization requires a culture where people can admit mistakes and still maintain their self-worth. The emphasis should be on learning and continuous improvement, not placing blame. A shared commitment to such values as trust, mutual respect, honesty, openness, cooperation, collaborative partnering, and taking responsibility for one's actions is essential to creating a more authentic culture. These values are also good for business.

Steps for Building a Values-Driven Organization

The following steps, based on the research findings summarized above, represent a blueprint for planning and implementing organizational culture change.

1) Gain top management support. You can prepare to do this by addressing the following questions:

   a) To whom would you like to make a proposal for culture change?

   b) What would you like to propose and why?

   c) Using research evidence and other relevant data, how can you build a persuasive case for culture assessment and change? (Note: data from activities described under step 2 below can be used for this purpose)

2) Assess current culture:

   a) Involve all stakeholder groups in the process, i.e. managers, employees, customers, and stockholders.

   b) Use a combination of instruments and interviews.

   c) Identify current purpose, vision, and goals.

   d) Identify underlying beliefs (assumptions, conclusions, and predictions that support current values (standards of importance), and current norms (standards for behavior) based on them.

   e) Decide which current purpose, vision, goals, beliefs, values, and norms you want to keep and which ones need to be change, by asking these questions:

      o What's working now and why?

      o What isn't working now and why?

      o How can you strengthen what's working, eliminate what isn't working, and change what needs to be fixed?

3) Define desired values:

   a) Involve all stakeholder groups in the process.

   b) Clarify new realities that make culture change necessary.

   c) Select values and practices that fit the organization's context, i.e. the needs of customers, the situation in labor markets, and the conditions in financial markets.

   d) Select values that emphasize all the key managerial constituencies (customers, employees, and stockholders), and leadership from managers at all levels.

   e) Include values that allow the organization to adapt to a changing environment.

f) Include values that emphasize short-term performance and efficiency, but don't compromise broader, long-range values.

g) Include values that pertain to the four key psychological and social needs of individuals and organizations: personal and social competence, and personal and social character.

h) Emphasize values that foster forward movement toward vision and goals, and eliminate or de-emphasize outmoded values.

4) Develop a set of norms based on the desired values. The norms should specify both acceptable behaviors (allowed) and unacceptable behaviors (not allowed).

5) Develop a plan for closing the gap between current and desired vision, goals, values, beliefs, and norms, and decide how it will be implemented.

6) Work toward alignment (compatibility) between personal and organizational vision, goals, values, so that the latter can become truly shared by addressing these questions:

a) What does the organization want (organizational interests)?

b) What do employees want (employee interests)?

c) In what ways are the wants compatible (aligned)?

d) How can areas of compatibility (alignment) be enhanced?

e) In what ways are the wants in conflict (misaligned)?

f) How can areas of conflict (misalignment) be reduced?

7) Embed desired values in management systems:

a) Initiate incremental changes in strategies and practices to keep the organization's values and norms in tune with environmental realities.

b) Align the values with vision, goals, strategies, tactics, and organizational design.

c) Use the values to guide strategic planning, make decisions, and set priorities.

d) Orient employees to the values.

e) Use the values to select employees, guide day-to-day actions and decisions, and evaluate performance.

f) Use the values to define criteria for advancement, and to set training and development objectives.

g) Build the reward system around the values.

h) Coach, counsel, and mentor for better fit between the values and behavior.

i) Hold everyone from top-down accountable for acting in accordance with the vision, goals, values, and norms.

8) Deal with resistance to change:

a) What resistance do you expect to these changes?

b) How can you overcome this resistance?

9) Work toward continuous improvement in aligning values with norms and practices.

10) Reassess the culture regularly.

Organizations are like ships on a stormy sea, battered on all sides by the winds of change. Values function as a rudder or, even better, as a compass. By ensuring that values are viable, balanced, congruent, and authentic, and by following the guidelines given above for building a values-driven culture, leaders and other change facilitators can help individuals, teams, and organizations successfully navigate the rough waters through which they must pass.

Value Assessment Tools

Two tools for assessing values are included at the end of this chapter: The Values Assessment Inventory™ (VAI) and the Values Identification Survey (VIS). Both tools have instructions for personal, team, and organizational uses, and include a 360-degree feedback option. The VAI assesses values according to the four criteria discussed in this chapter.

The Values Identification Survey can be used for the following:

- To identify the actual values of individuals, teams, and organizations;
- To establish desired personal, team, and organizational values;
- To make the following comparisons among personal, team, and organizational values:

Personal Values

To compare actual with desired personal values

To compare personal with actual team values

To compare personal with actual organizational values

To compare self, supervisor, peer, and subordinate perceptions of current personal values

Team Values

To compare actual with espoused team values

To compare actual with desired team values

To compare actual team with actual organizational values

Organizational Values

To compare actual with espoused organizational values

To compare actual with desired organizational values

VALUES ASSESSMENT INVENTORY™

PURPOSE: To assess current individual, team, or organizational values according to four variables necessary for effective functioning: balance, viability, alignment, and authenticity (60 items).

Introduction

Four variables determine the overall effectiveness of a team or organization's value system, which can be defined as follows:

- **Balance**—the degree to which values are given proper emphasis.

- **Viability**—the degree to which values are workable in the current business climate.

- **Alignment (congruence)**—the degree to which compatibility exists among an individual's values, or among the values of individuals, teams, and the overall organization.

- **Authenticity**—the degree to which values are used in a genuine, sincere manner.

The VAI (Regular Form) provides a general assessment of current personal, team, and organizational values, while the VAI (360° Feedback Form) allows individuals to compare self, supervisor, peer and subordinate value ratings. Mean scores can range from 0 to 60. High mean scores show that values are effective, while low mean scores show that values are ineffective. Scores less than 30 should be viewed as cause for concern. Also, even if the mean score for a variable is high, items consistently receiving scores of 0 or 1 indicate problems. The VAI can be completed by itself or in conjunction with the Values Identification Survey and/or Motivational System Mapping™.

Procedures for Organizational Use

The VAI (Regular Form) can be copied and given to everyone in an organization, to a representative sample, or to members of the leadership team. Check the YOUR ORGANIZATION box on the first page so respondents understand that the *overall organization* is the focus of assessment. Inform respondents that their results will be confidential. Follow the instructions for calculating scores. Then meet with organizational leaders, display the completed Values Assessment Profile, facilitate a discussion of the results, and develop strategies for dealing with organizational values issues.

Procedures for Team Use

The VAI (Regular Form) can be copied and given to everyone on a team to assess current team values. Check the YOUR TEAM box on the front page so respondents understand that the *team* is the focus of assessment. Inform respondents that their results will be confidential. Follow the instructions for calculating scores. Then meet with the team, display the completed Values Assessment Profile, facilitate a discussion of the results, and develop strategies for dealing with team values issues.

Procedures for Personal Use

The VAI (Regular Form) can be copied and completed by individuals to assess their current values. He or she should check the YOURSELF box on the front page, respond to the 60 items, calculate their scores, and place the scores on the Values Assessment Profile. Following this, the person should examine the Profile, reflect on the results, and develop strategies for dealing with personal values issues.

Procedures for 360° Feedback

The VAI (360° Feedback Form) can be copied and used with an individual to compare self, supervisor, peer and subordinate ratings. When administering the inventory, a sample of peers and all subordinates should be included. A cover letter should be provided to those in the sample, indicating the person to be evaluated, the purpose of the assessment, and where to return completed inventories. Inform respondents that their results will remain confidential. Follow the instructions for calculating scores. Then meet with the individual, review the completed Values Assessment Profile, discuss similarities and differences among self, supervisor, peer and subordinate ratings, and develop strategies for dealing with individual values issues.

Values Assessment Inventory™
(Regular Form)

by
Ken Hultman

Name: _____   Date: _____

Position: _____

Team: _____

Organization: _____

NOTE: As you complete this inventory you will be rating (check one):
☐ **Yourself,** ☐ **Your team, or** ☐ **Your organization**

Instructions

The Values Assessment Inventory™ allows you to evaluate the effectiveness of values in the current business climate.

Read each item and circle the response that best expresses your opinion. The scale is a continuum from 0 to 4, with 0 meaning strongly disagree and 4 meaning strongly agree (Note: a few items are reverse scored due to the phrasing of questions).

These are tough questions, requiring careful thought and introspection. Please give your honest opinions; otherwise the results will be meaningless. Team and organizational ratings will be grouped together and remain anonymous.

THANK YOU FOR COMPLETING THIS INVENTORY

please turn the page and begin ⇒

	Strongly Disagree				Strongly Agree

Balance

1.	Avoid taking extreme positions on issues.	0	1	2	3	4
2.	Objectively weigh other's views.	0	1	2	3	4
3.	Emphasize some aspects of work at the expense of others.	4	3	2	1	0
4.	Compromise on issues when appropriate.	0	1	2	3	4
5.	Keep an open mind when opinions differ.	0	1	2	3	4
6.	Emphasize mutual interests.	0	1	2	3	4
7.	Maintain balance between tasks and people.	0	1	2	3	4
8.	Maintain balance between work and home.	0	1	2	3	4
9.	Place too little emphasis on some needs.	4	3	2	1	0
10.	Take a reasonable position on issues.	0	1	2	3	4
11.	Balance short-term and long-range needs.	0	1	2	3	4
12.	Show a willingness to be flexible.	0	1	2	3	4
13.	Present opinions dogmatically.	4	3	2	1	0
14.	Have symptoms of burn out.	4	3	2	1	0
15.	Pay attention to all important needs.	0	1	2	3	4

TOTAL FOR BALANCE: _____

Viability

16.	Place a priority on learning.	0	1	2	3	4
17.	Give others the benefit of the doubt.	0	1	2	3	4
18.	Treat others like persons, not numbers.	0	1	2	3	4
19.	Have difficulty adapting to change.	4	3	2	1	0
20.	Show a desire for growth.	0	1	2	3	4
21.	Consider the consequences of decisions.	0	1	2	3	4
22.	Think "outside the box."	0	1	2	3	4
23.	Demonstrate creativity and innovativeness.	0	1	2	3	4
24.	Long for the "good old days."	4	3	2	1	0
25.	Emphasize personal development.	0	1	2	3	4
26.	Take appropriate risks.	0	1	2	3	4
27.	Articulate values clearly.	0	1	2	3	4

	Strongly Disagree				Strongly Agree

28. Get effective results. 0 1 2 3 4
29. Back up opinions with data. 0 1 2 3 4
30. Encourage others to grow. 0 1 2 3 4

TOTAL FOR VIABILITY: _____

Congruence

31. Choose behaviors consistent with values. 0 1 2 3 4
32. Have a compatible set of values. 0 1 2 3 4
33. Convey the same message to everyone. 0 1 2 3 4
34. Walk the talk. 0 1 2 3 4
35. Effectively match methods with goals. 0 1 2 3 4
36. Keep changing positions on issues. 4 3 2 1 0
37. Identify and manage tradeoffs effectively. 0 1 2 3 4
38. Disagree with others about goals/methods. 4 3 2 1 0
39. Agree with others about priorities. 0 1 2 3 4
40. Stand up for convictions. 0 1 2 3 4
41. Resist pressures to conform. 0 1 2 3 4
42. Honor commitments. 0 1 2 3 4
43. Remain steadfast in the face of opposition. 0 1 2 3 4
44. Don't impose values on others. 0 1 2 3 4
45. Avoid waffling on issues. 0 1 2 3 4

TOTAL FOR CONGRUENCE: _____

Authenticity

46. Use manipulative tactics. 4 3 2 1 0
47. Have hidden agendas. 4 3 2 1 0
48. Have a commitment to the truth. 0 1 2 3 4
49. Respond in a non-defensive manner. 0 1 2 3 4
50. Pretend to agree with others. 4 3 2 1 0
51. Don't take advantage of others. 0 1 2 3 4
52. Share information freely. 0 1 2 3 4
53. Focus on placing blame. 4 3 2 1 0
54. Distort what others say. 4 3 2 1 0

	Strongly Disagree				Strongly Agree
55. Take responsibility for mistakes.	0	1	2	3	4
56. Face issues openly and honestly.	0	1	2	3	4
57. Gossip about others.	4	3	2	1	0
58. Avoid responding in anger.	0	1	2	3	4
59. Don't gloat over other's misfortunes.	0	1	2	3	4
60. Can be trusted.	0	1	2	3	4

TOTAL FOR AUTHENTICITY: _____

Instructions for Completing the Values Assessment Profile

If you are rating yourself, place a dot at the corresponding point for the 4 total scores listed above (balance, viability, congruence, and authenticity), and connect the dots with a line. If you are rating your team or organization, add the totals of all respondents together for each variable and divide these scores by the number of respondents completing the inventory. This will give you the average or mean scores for the four variables.

Values Assessment Profile

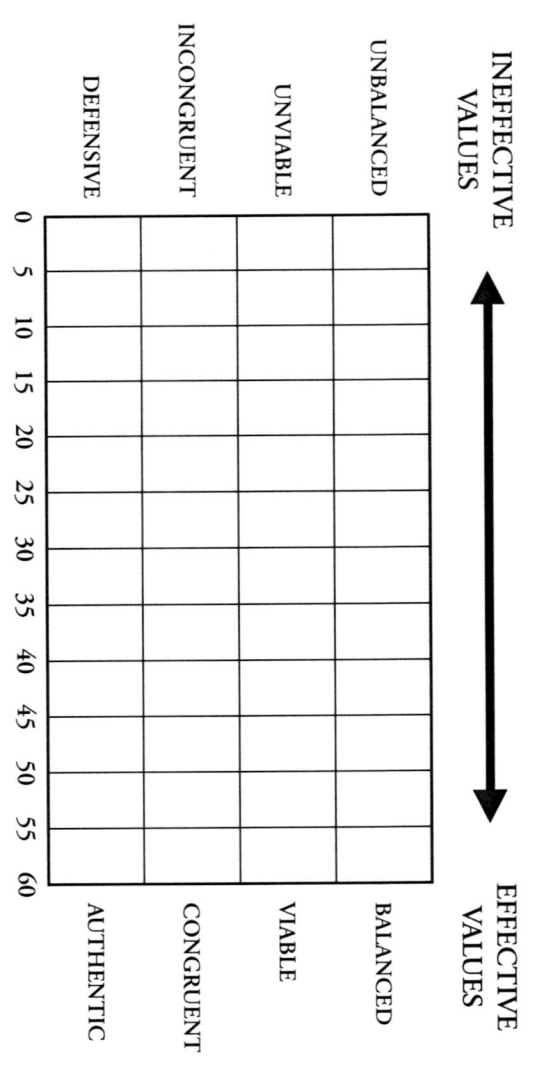

INEFFECTIVE VALUES — EFFECTIVE VALUES

	0	5	10	15	20	25	30	35	40	45	50	55	60	
UNBALANCED														BALANCED
UNVIABLE														VIABLE
INCONGRUENT														CONGRUENT
DEFENSIVE														AUTHENTIC

Values Assessment Inventory™
(360° Feedback Form)

by
Ken Hultman

Name: _____   Date: _____

Position: _____

Team: _____

Organization: _____

NOTE: As you complete this inventory your ratings will be for the following person:

_____

Instructions

The *Values Assessment* Inventory™—360° Feedback Version is a developmental tool intended to help people evaluate the effectiveness of their values in the current business climate.

Read each item and circle the response that best applies to the person named above. The scale is a continuum from 0 to 4, with 0 meaning strongly disagree and 4 meaning strongly agree (Note: a few items are reverse scored due to the phrasing of questions).

These are tough questions, requiring careful thought and introspection. Please give your honest opinions; otherwise the results will be meaningless. Peer and subordinate ratings will be grouped together and will remain anonymous.

THANK YOU FOR COMPLETING THIS INVENTORY

please turn the page and begin ⇒

	Strongly Disagree				Strongly Agree

Balance

1.	Avoids taking extreme positions on issues.	0	1	2	3	4
2.	Objectively weighs other's views.	0	1	2	3	4
3.	Emphasizes some aspects of work at the expense of others.	4	3	2	1	0
4.	Compromises on issues when appropriate.	0	1	2	3	4
5.	Keeps an open mind when opinions differ.	0	1	2	3	4
6.	Emphasizes mutual interests.	0	1	2	3	4
7.	Maintains balance between tasks and people.	0	1	2	3	4
8.	Maintains balance between work and home.	0	1	2	3	4
9.	Places too little emphasis on some needs.	4	3	2	1	0
10.	Takes a reasonable position on issues.	0	1	2	3	4
11.	Balances short-term and long-range needs.	0	1	2	3	4
12.	Shows a willingness to be flexible.	0	1	2	3	4
13.	Presents opinions dogmatically.	4	3	2	1	0
14.	Has symptoms of burn out.	4	3	2	1	0
15.	Pays attention to all important needs.	0	1	2	3	4

TOTAL FOR BALANCE: _____

Viability

16.	Places a priority on learning.	0	1	2	3	4
17.	Gives others the benefit of the doubt.	0	1	2	3	4
18.	Treats others like persons, not numbers.	0	1	2	3	4
19.	Has difficulty adapting to change.	4	3	2	1	0
20.	Shows a desire for growth.	0	1	2	3	4
21.	Considers the consequences of decisions.	0	1	2	3	4
22.	Thinks "outside the box."	0	1	2	3	4
23.	Demonstrates creativity and innovativeness.	0	1	2	3	4
24.	Longs for the "good old days."	4	3	2	1	0
25.	Emphasizes personal development.	0	1	2	3	4
26.	Takes appropriate risks.	0	1	2	3	4
27.	Articulates values clearly.	0	1	2	3	4

	Strongly Disagree				Strongly Agree

28.	Gets effective results.	0	1	2	3	4
29.	Backs up opinions with data.	0	1	2	3	4
30.	Encourages others to grow.	0	1	2	3	4

TOTAL FOR VIABILITY:_____

Congruence

31.	Chooses behaviors consistent with values.	0	1	2	3	4
32.	Has a compatible set of values.	0	1	2	3	4
33.	Conveys the same message to everyone.	0	1	2	3	4
34.	Walks the talk.	0	1	2	3	4
35.	Effectively matches methods with goals.	0	1	2	3	4
36.	Keeps changing positions on issues.	4	3	2	1	0
37.	Identifies and manages tradeoffs effectively.	0	1	2	3	4
38.	Disagrees with others about goals/methods.	4	3	2	1	0
39.	Agrees with others about priorities.	0	1	2	3	4
40.	Stands up for convictions.	0	1	2	3	4
41.	Resists pressures to conform.	0	1	2	3	4
42.	Honors commitments.	0	1	2	3	4
43.	Remains steadfast in the face of opposition.	0	1	2	3	4
44.	Doesn't impose values on others.	0	1	2	3	4
45.	Avoids waffling on issues.	0	1	2	3	4

TOTAL FOR CONGRUENCE:_____

Authenticity

46.	Uses manipulative tactics.	4	3	2	1	0
47.	Has hidden agendas.	4	3	2	1	0
48.	Has a commitment to the truth.	0	1	2	3	4
49.	Responds in a non-defensive manner.	0	1	2	3	4
50.	Pretends to agree with others.	4	3	2	1	0
51.	Doesn't take advantage of others.	0	1	2	3	4
52.	Shares information freely.	0	1	2	3	4
53.	Focuses on placing blame.	4	3	2	1	0
54.	Distorts what others say.	4	3	2	1	0

	Strongly Disagree				Strongly Agree
55. Takes responsibility for mistakes.	0	1	2	3	4
56. Faces issues openly and honestly.	0	1	2	3	4
57. Gossips about others.	4	3	2	1	0
58. Avoids responding in anger.	0	1	2	3	4
59. Doesn't gloat over other's misfortunes.	0	1	2	3	4
60. Can be trusted.	0	1	2	3	4

TOTAL FOR AUTHENTICITY: _____

Instructions for Completing the Values Assessment Profile

There are four types of ratings that should be placed on the Profile: self, supervisor, peer, and subordinate (Note: color code the four types of ratings, so they can be distinguished from each other).

- Self-ratings can be listed by placing a dot at the corresponding point for the 4 total scores (balance, viability, congruence, and authenticity), and connecting the dots with a line. The same procedure can be used for supervisor ratings, if one supervisor completed the inventory (If more than one supervisor responded, use the procedures outlined below for peers and subordinates).

- Peer ratings can be listed by adding the totals of all peers together for each variable, and dividing these scores by the number of peers responding. This will give you the average or mean scores for peers. The same procedure can be used for subordinates.

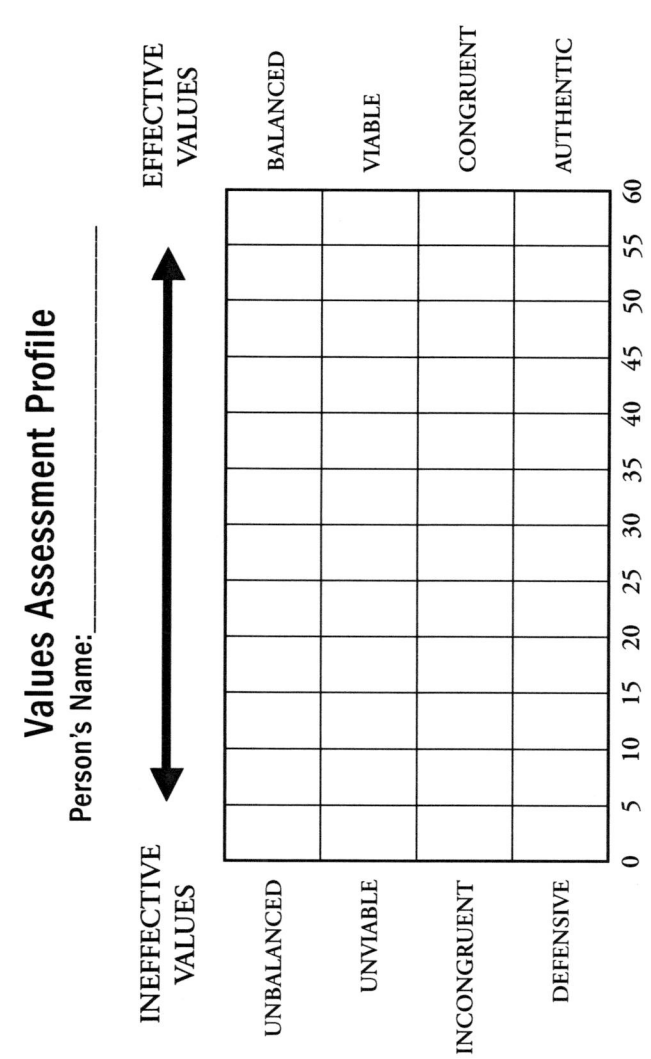

Values Assessment Profile
Person's Name: _____

VALUES IDENTIFICATION SURVEY

PURPOSE: To identify the actual values of teams, organizations, and individuals, make a variety of comparisons among organizational, team, and individual values, and establish team or organizational values.

Introduction

The purpose of the Values Identification Survey (VIS) is to clarify the values of individuals, teams, and organizations. The VIS consists of three forms, Actual Values, Espoused Values and Desired Values, each containing a list of 185 values in alphabetical order. This list is not intended to be exhaustive, so space is provided on each form to write in other values. The three types of values are defined as follows:

- **Actual Values**—standards that guide behavior currently.
- **Espoused Values**—standards that people say they value.
- **Desired Values**—standards that people would like to have guide behavior.

The VIS can be administered by itself, or in conjunction with the Values Assessment Inventory™ and Motivational System Mapping™ to assess and deal with values issues.

Instructions

The VIS has a number of personal, team, and organizational uses that are keyed to detailed instruction sheets. The instruction sheets allow a facilitator to consolidate data, assess values, and conduct feedback meetings where values are discussed and decisions regarding values are made. To accomplish these tasks, the facilitator should:

- Follow the procedures for organizational, team, personal, and 360° feedback uses.
- Consolidate data and complete steps 1 and 2 on the appropriate instruction sheet.
- Make copies of the instruction sheet and distribute them at the beginning of a feedback session.
- Summarize the data and answer questions.
- Facilitate discussion pertaining to the remaining steps on the instruction sheet.

Table 7.10 summarizes the materials needed for various uses of the VIS at the personal, team, and organizational levels.

Table 7.10

Materials Needed for Using the VIS with Individuals, Teams, and Organizations

LEVEL→ / USES↓	INDIVIDUAL	TEAM	ORGANIZATION
Identify actual values	Actual Values Form for a person *Instruction Sheet #1*	Actual Values Form for a team *Instruction Sheet #1*	Actual Values Form for an organization *Instruction Sheet #1*
Establish values	Desired Values Form for a person *Instruction Sheet #2*	Desired Values Form for a team *Instruction Sheet #2*	Desired Values Form for an organization *Instruction Sheet #2*
Compare actual with espoused values		Actual Values Form and Espoused Values Forms for a team *Instruction Sheet #3*	Actual Values Form and Espoused Values Form for an organization *Instruction Sheet #3*
Compare actual with desired values	Actual Values Form and Desired Values Form for a person *Instruction Sheet #4*	Actual Values Form and Desired Values Form for a team *Instruction Sheet #4*	Actual Values Form and Desired Values Form for an organization *Instruction Sheet #4*
Compare personal with team values	Actual Values Form for a person and Actual Values Forms for a team *Instruction Sheet #5*		
Compare personal with organizational values	Actual Values Form for a person and Actual Values Forms for an organization *Instruction Sheet #5*		
360° feedback	Actual Values Form for self, supervisor, peers, and subordinates *Instruction Sheet #6*		
Compare actual team with actual organizational values		Actual Values Form for a team and Actual Values Form for an organization *Instruction Sheet #5*	

Procedures for Organizational Use

The Actual Values Form can be used by itself to identify current organizational values, or in conjunction with (1) the Espoused Values Form to compare current with verbally touted organizational values, or (2) the

Desired Values Form to compare current with ideal organizational values. The Desired Form can be used by itself to establish organizational values.

The VIS can be given to everyone in an organization, to a representative sample, or to members of the leadership team. Check the appropriate box on the first page of the VIS form(s), and distribute them as appropriate. Then follow the instructions for listing results and facilitating discussion.

Procedures for Team Use

The Actual Values Form can be used by itself to identify current team values, or in conjunction with (1) the Espoused Values Form to compare current with verbally touted team values, (2) the Desired Values Form to compare current with ideal team values, or (3) the Actual Values Form for organizations to compare current team and organizational values. The Desired Form can be used by itself to establish team values.

Check the appropriate box on the front page of the VIS form(s), and distribute them to team members. Then follow the instructions for listing results and facilitating discussion.

Procedures for Individual Use

The Actual Values Form can be used by itself to identify current personal values, or in conjunction with (1) the Desired Values Form to compare current with desired personal values, (2) the Actual Values Form for a team to compare current personal and team values, or (3) the Actual Values Form for an organization to compare current personal and organizational values. Also, the Desired Values Form can be used by itself to establish desired personal values.

Check the appropriate box on the front page on the VIS form(s), and distribute them as appropriate. Then follow the instructions for listing results and facilitating discussion.

Procedures for 360° Feedback

The Actual Values Form can be used to compare self, supervisor, peer and subordinate perceptions of current individual values. When conducting this assessment, a sample of peers and all subordinates should be included. A cover letter should be provided to those in the sample, indicating the purpose of the assessment and where to return completed surveys.

Write the person's name on the front page of the Actual Values Form, so respondents understand who is the focus of assessment. Summarize results on Instruction Sheet #6. Then meet with the individual and review the findings, discuss similarities and differences among self, supervisor, peer and subordinate perceptions, and develop strategies for dealing with identified values issues.

Values Identification Survey
(Actual Values)

NAME: _____   POSITION: _____

ORGANIZATION: _____   TEAM: _____   DATE: _____

Instructions: Circle the 10 most important values that actually guide (check one):

☐ Your Team's Behavior, ☐ Your Organization's Behavior, ☐ Your Behavior, or
☐ The Behavior of (Person's Name): _____

Accepting others	Dedication	Individuality	Profitability
Accomplishment	Deference	Influence	Progress
Accountability	Delight	Initiative	Quality
Achievement	Dependability	Innovation	Recognition
Adaptability	Developing others	Integrity	Relationships
Adding value	Dignity	Intelligence	Reliability
Advancement	Diligence	Interdependent	Respect
Adventure	Diplomacy	Intuition	Responsibility
Affirmation	Discretion	Involvement	Responsiveness
Alignment	Diversity	Justice	Results
Ambition	Effectiveness	Kindness	Risk-taking
Approval	Efficiency	Knowledge	Routine
A sense of community	Empowerment	Law abiding	Security
Assertiveness	Enthusiasm	Learning	Self-control
Authenticity	Environmentalism	Logical	Self-interest
Authority	Ethics	Love	Self-discipline
Balance home/work	Equality	Loyalty	Self-respect
Belonging	Excellence	Making a difference	Self-starter
Boundaryless	Expediency	Mastery	Seniority
Candor	Fairness	Material possessions	Service
Caring	Faith	Mentoring	Sincerity
Caution	Faithfulness	Mercy	Social awareness
Clean	Fellowship	Merit	Speed
Cohesiveness	Financial growth	Morality	Spirituality
Collaboration	Flexibility	Mutual interests	Spontaneity
Comfort	Forgiveness	Networking	Stability
Commitment	Friendship	Obedience	Status
Community involvement	Freedom	Openness	Status quo
Companionship	Generosity	Opportunity	Stewardship
Compassion	Genuineness	Optimism	Strategic focus
Competence	Giving something back	Order	Success
Competition	Glory	Organizational growth	Synergism
Confidentiality	Good will	Originality	Tact
Congruence	Growth	Ownership	Teamwork
Consistency	Harmony	Participation	Territory
Contribution	Health	Partnering	Timeliness
Control	Helpfulness	Patience	Tolerance
Cooperation	Honesty	Peace	Tradition
Coordination	Honor	Perseverance	Trust
Courtesy	Humanitarianism	Philanthropy	Truth
Courage	Humility	Politeness	Variety
Creativity	Humor/fun	Popularity	Volunteerism
Credentials	Imagination	Power	Willpower
Credibility	Improvement	Prestige	Winning
Curiosity	Inclusiveness	Productivity	Wisdom
Customer satisfaction	Independence	Professionalism	Other: _____

Values Identification Survey
(Espoused Values)

NAME: _____   POSITION: _____

ORGANIZATION: _____   TEAM: _____   DATE: _____

Instructions: Circle the 10 most important values verbally espoused in (check one):

☐ Your team   ☐ Your organization

Accepting others	Dedication	Individuality	Profitability
Accomplishment	Deference	Influence	Progress
Accountability	Delight	Initiative	Quality
Achievement	Dependability	Innovation	Recognition
Adaptability	Developing others	Integrity	Relationships
Adding value	Dignity	Intelligence	Reliability
Advancement	Diligence	Interdependent	Respect
Adventure	Diplomacy	Intuition	Responsibility
Affirmation	Discretion	Involvement	Responsiveness
Alignment	Diversity	Justice	Results
Ambition	Effectiveness	Kindness	Risk-taking
Approval	Efficiency	Knowledge	Routine
A sense of community	Empowerment	Law abiding	Security
Assertiveness	Enthusiasm	Learning	Self-control
Authenticity	Environmentalism	Logical	Self-interest
Authority	Ethics	Love	Self-discipline
Balance home/work	Equality	Loyalty	Self-respect
Belonging	Excellence	Making a difference	Seniority
Boundaryless	Expediency	Mastery	Service
Candor	Fairness	Material possessions	Sincerity
Caring	Faith	Mentoring	Social awareness
Caution	Faithfulness	Mercy	Speed
Clean	Fellowship	Merit	Spirituality
Cohesiveness	Financial growth	Morality	Spontaneity
Collaboration	Flexibility	Mutual interest	Stability
Comfort	Forgiveness	Networking	Status
Commitment	Friendship	Obedience	Status quo
Community involvement	Freedom	Openness	Stewardship
Companionship	Generosity	Opportunity	Strategic focus
Compassion	Genuineness	Optimism	Success
Competence	Giving something back	Order	Synergism
Competition	Glory	Organizational growth	Tact
Confidentiality	Good will	Originality	Teamwork
Congruence	Growth	Ownership	Territory
Consistency	Harmony	Participation	Timeliness
Contribution	Health	Partnering	Tolerance
Control	Helpfulness	Patience	Tradition
Cooperation	Honesty	Peace	Trust
Coordination	Honor	Perseverance	Truth
Courtesy	Humanitarianism	Philanthropy	Variety
Courage	Humility	Politeness	Volunteerism
Creativity	Humor/fun	Popularity	Willpower
Credentials	Imagination	Power	Winning
Credibility	Improvement	Prestige	Wisdom
Curiosity	Inclusiveness	Productivity	Other:
Customer satisfaction	Independence	Professionalism	

Values Identification Survey
(Desired Values)

NAME: _____   POSITION: _____

ORGANIZATION: _____   TEAM: _____   DATE: _____

Instructions: Circle the 10 most important values you would like to have guide behavior for (check one):

☐ Yourself   ☐ Your team   ☐ Your organization

Accepting others	Dedication	Individuality	Profitability
Accomplishment	Deference	Influence	Progress
Accountability	Delight	Initiative	Quality
Achievement	Dependability	Innovation	Recognition
Adaptability	Developing others	Integrity	Relationships
Adding value	Dignity	Intelligence	Reliability
Advancement	Diligence	Interdependent	Respect
Adventure	Diplomacy	Intuition	Responsibility
Affirmation	Discretion	Involvement	Responsiveness
Alignment	Diversity	Justice	Results
Ambition	Effectiveness	Kindness	Risk-taking
Approval	Efficiency	Knowledge	Routine
A sense of community	Empowerment	Law abiding	Security
Assertiveness	Enthusiasm	Learning	Self-control
Authenticity	Environmentalism	Logical	Self-interest
Authority	Ethics	Love	Self-discipline
Balance home/work	Equality	Loyalty	Self-respect
Belonging	Excellence	Making a difference	Self-starter
Boundaryless	Expediency	Mastery	Seniority
Candor	Fairness	Material possessions	Service
Caring	Faith	Mentoring	Sincerity
Caution	Faithfulness	Mercy	Social awareness
Clean	Fellowship	Merit	Speed
Cohesiveness	Financial growth	Morality	Spirituality
Collaboration	Flexibility	Mutual interests	Spontaneity
Comfort	Forgiveness	Networking	Stability
Commitment	Friendship	Obedience	Status
Community involvement	Freedom	Openness	Status quo
Companionship	Generosity	Opportunity	Stewardship
Compassion	Genuineness	Optimism	Strategic focus
Competence	Giving something back	Order	Success
Competition	Glory	Organizational growth	Synergism
Confidentiality	Good will	Originality	Tact
Congruence	Growth	Ownership	Teamwork
Consistency	Harmony	Participation	Territory
Contribution	Health	Partnering	Timeliness
Control	Helpfulness	Patience	Tolerance
Cooperation	Honesty	Peace	Tradition
Coordination	Honor	Perseverance	Trust
Courtesy	Humanitarianism	Philanthropy	Truth
Courage	Humility	Politeness	Variety
Creativity	Humor/fun	Popularity	Volunteerism
Credentials	Imagination	Power	Willpower
Credibility	Improvement	Prestige	Winning
Curiosity	Inclusiveness	Productivity	Wisdom
Customer satisfaction	Independence	Professionalism	Other: _____

Values Identification Survey
Instruction Sheet #1

USE: To identify Actual Values for:

☐ **Your Organization**   ☐ **Your Team**   ☐ **Yourself**

1. **LIST** the top ten Actual Values. (Note: List an individual's values in alphabetical order; list a team or organization's values in rank order, indicating how many people selected each one).

    Actual Values:

    1.
    2.
    3.
    4.
    5.
    6.
    7.
    8.
    9.
    10.

2. **LABEL** each value according to its function: defensive (D), which focus on protecting against perceived threat; stabilizing (S), which focus on maintaining the status quo; or growth (G), which provide for forward movement.

3. **EVALUATE** the values according to the following criteria:

    BALANCE

    Are there values pertaining to all four needs (mastery, contribution, self-respect, acceptance)?

    VIABILITY

    Are the values workable in the current business climate?

    How can defensive and stabilizing values be decreased?

    How can growth values be increased?

    ALIGNMENT

    Are the values compatible with one another?

    AUTHENTICITY

    Are the values used in a genuine, sincere manner?

4. **DECIDE** on changes needed with Actual Values and how these changes will be made.

Values Identification Survey
Instruction Sheet #2

USE: To establish Desired Values for:

☐ **Your Organization**   ☐ **Your Team**   ☐ **Yourself**

1. **LIST** the top ten Desired Values in rank order (indicating how many people selected each one in case of team or organizational rankings).

Desired Values:

1.
2.
3.
4.
5.
6.
7.
8.
9.
10.

2. **LABEL** each value according to its function: defensive (D), which focus on protecting against perceived threat; stabilizing (S), which focus on maintaining the status quo; or growth (G), which provide for forward movement.

3. **EVALUATE** the values according to the following criteria:

BALANCE

Are there values pertaining to all four needs (mastery, contribution, self-respect, acceptance)?

VIABILITY

Are the values workable in the current business climate?

How can defensive and stabilizing values be decreased?

How can growth values be increased?

ALIGNMENT

Are the values compatible with one another?

AUTHENTICITY

Are the values used in a genuine, sincere manner?

4. **DECIDE** on final list of values and develop behavioral definitions.

Values Identification Survey
Instruction Sheet #3

USE: To compare Actual with Espoused Values for:

□ **Your Organization**   □ **Your Team**

1. **LIST** the top ten Actual and Espoused Values in rank order, indicating how many people selected each one.

Actual Values for:	Espoused Values for:
1.	1.
2.	2.
3.	3.
4.	4.
5.	5.
6.	6.
7.	7.
8.	8.
9.	9.
10.	10.

2. **LABEL** each value according to its function: defensive (D), which focus on protecting against perceived threat; stabilizing (S), which focus on maintaining the status quo; or growth (G), which provide for forward movement.

3. **COMPARE** the similarities and differences between Actual and Espoused Values.

4. **DISCUSS** how to bring about greater alignment between Actual and Espoused Values.

5. **LAYOUT** goals, objectives, and plans for improving alignment.

Values Identification Survey
Instruction Sheet #4

USE: To compare Actual with Desired Values for:

☐ Your Organization   ☐ Your Team   ☐ Yourself

1. **LIST** the top ten Actual and Desired Values in rank order (indicating how many people selected each one in case of team or organizational ranking).

Actual Values for:

1.
2.
3.
4.
5.
6.
7.
8.
9.
10.

Desired Values for:

1.
2.
3.
4.
5.
6.
7.
8.
9.
10.

2. **LABEL** each value according to its function: Defensive (D), which focus on protecting against perceived threat; Stabilizing (S), which focus on maintaining the status quo; or Growth (G), which provide for forward movement.

3. **COMPARE** the similarities and differences between Actual and Desired Values.

4. **DISCUSS** how to get from Actual to Desired Values.

How can Defensive and Stabilizing Values be decreased?

How can Growth Values be increased?

5. **LAYOUT** goals, objectives, and plans for moving toward Desired Values.

Values Identification Survey
Instruction Sheet #5

USE: To compare Actual Values between:

☐ **Yourself and your team**

☐ **Yourself and your organization**

☐ **Your team and your organization**

1. **LIST** the two sets of top ten Actual Values for the comparison checked above (NOTE: if the comparison is between yourself and your team or organization, list your values in alphabetical order and the team or organization's values in rank order, indicating how many people selected each one. If the comparison is between your team and organization, list the values in rank order).

Actual Values:	**Actual Values:**
1.	1.
2.	2.
3.	3.
4.	4.
5.	5.
6.	6.
7.	7.
8.	8.
9.	9.
10.	10.

2. **LABEL** each value according to its function: defensive (D), which focus on protecting against perceived threat; stabilizing (S), which focus on maintaining the status quo; or growth (G), which provide for forward movement.

3. **COMPARE** the similarities and differences between Actual Values.

4. **DISCUSS** how to bring about greater alignment among Actual Values.

5. **LAYOUT** goals, objectives, and plans for increasing alignment.

Values Identification Survey
Instruction Sheet #6

USE: To compare self, supervisor, peer and subordinate perceptions of Actual Values for (Person's Name):

1. **LIST** the top ten values for self, supervisor, peers and subordinates (NOTE: List self and supervisor values in alphabetical order, but list peer and subordinate values in rank order, indicating how many people selected each one).

Self:	Supervisor:	Peer:	Subordinate:
1.	1.	1.	1.
2.	2.	2.	2.
3.	3.	3.	3.
4.	4.	4.	4.
5.	5.	5.	5.
6.	6.	6.	6.
7.	7.	7.	7.
8.	8.	8.	8.
9.	9.	9.	9.
10.	10,	10.	10.

2. **LABEL** each value according to its function: defensive (D), which focus on protecting against perceived threat; stabilizing (S), which focus on maintaining the status quo; or growth (G), which provide for forward movement.

3. **COMPARE** the similarities and differences between self, supervisor, peer and subordinate perceptions of values.

4. **DISCUSS** on value changes needed and how these changes will be made.
   How can defensive and stabilizing values be decreased?
   How can growth values be increased?

5. **LAYOUT** goals, objectives, and plans for value changes.

8

REMOVING BARRIERS TO ORGANIZATIONAL EFFECTIVENESS

PURPOSE: To describe a systems approach to motivation that can be used with individuals, teams, and organizations to assess their current situation and make change decisions.

Introduction

Motivation is concerned with the question, *"Why do people do what they do?"* Organization development (OD) practitioners have a keen interest in motivation, because much of their work centers around three questions:

1. What are people doing currently and *why?*
2. What do they want to be doing instead and *why?* and
3. How can they get from the current to the desired?

Various motivational theories have been offered by psychologists and other behavioral scientists over the last 50 years. As a body of literature, these theories have focused principally on five variables: needs, thinking (cognition), feelings (emotions), deciding (valuing), and doing (behavior). The five variables can be defined as follows:

- **Needs:** Urges or desires originating within us. People's have physical, personal, social, and spiritual needs.

- **Thinking:** Using one's mind, taking in information and interpreting it. The key factors in the thinking process are.

  - **Facts:** Objective realities that can be proven with empirical evidence.

  - **Beliefs:** Subjective assumption, conclusion, or prediction.

- **Feeling:** Our emotions

- **Deciding:** Using one's will, making up one's mind, choosing. Choices are based on values, which are standards of importance based on beliefs about what's important in life. Values serve as criteria for making decisions and setting priorities.

- **Doing:** Actions or behaviors based on needs, facts, beliefs, feelings, and values.

In the process of meeting our needs, we think, we feel, we decide, and we do. These variables all interact in complex ways, contributing to what we call *motivation*. Table 8.1 shows the relationship between the five variables and selected theories/processes of personal and organizational change (Note: this is not intended to be an exhaustive list). It also underscores OD's interdisciplinary roots; in one way or another, most of these approaches have been adapted for OD purposes.

Table 8.1

Relationship between Five Motivational Variables and Selected Theories/Processes of Personal and Organizational Change

Motivational Variables	Selected Theories/Processes of Personal and Organizational Change	
NEEDS (drives, urges)	Maslow's need hierarchy	
	Herzberg's motivational theory	
	McClelland's acquired needs for achievement, affiliation, and power	
	Alderfer's ERG theory	
	Psychoanalytic theory	
	Self-determination theory	
THINKING (facts, beliefs, perceptions)	Expectancy theory	Bion's theory of group dynamics
	Consistency theory	
	Personal construct psychology	
	Gestalt therapy	
	Cognitive-behavioral therapy	
	Rational-emotive therapy	
	McGregor's Theory X and Theory Y	
	Bandura's perceived self-efficacy Theory	
FEELINGS (emotions)	Emotional intelligence	Stress management
	Client-centered psychotherapy	Meditation
	Personal growth groups (T-groups)	
	Appreciative Inquiry	
	Primal therapy	
	Psychodrama	
	Systematic desensitization, *in vivo* desensitization, implosive therapy, flooding	

Motivational Variables	Selected Theories/Processes of Personal and Organizational Change
DECIDING (values)	Values clarification
	Affective education
	Awareness building
	Equity theory
	Path-goal theory
	Exchange theory
	Psychological contract
	Strategic planning
	Cost/benefit analysis
	Envisioning
	Culture assessment and change
	Normative OD approaches
	Values-based leadership
	Participative management
	Spirituality in the workplace
	Jacques' cognitive complexity theory
DOING (behavior)	Classical and operant conditioning
	Behavior therapy
	Organizational behavior modification
	Reinforcement theory
	Social learning theory
	Behavior modeling
	Role playing with feedback
	Management by objectives (MBO)
	Benchmarking
	Empowerment
	Process improvement (TQM, CQI, etc.)
	Downsizing, re-engineering

While these theories or processes rarely pay exclusive attention to one variable, they do tend to emphasize one or two over the others. For example, Maslow's work concentrated on needs and values, but he's most widely known for his hierarchy of needs. Gestalt therapy emphasizes thinking (perception and beliefs) and behavior. Cognitive-behavioral therapy look at both thinking and doing, but the focus is on changing beliefs in order to bring about behavior change. Behavioral therapy focuses on doing, arguing that it's unnecessary to even postulate the existence of beliefs and values. Management by objectives sets goals based on thinking and deciding, but the primary thrust is toward putting those goals into concrete action (behavior).

In addition, most motivational theories contend that one or two variables are causes while others are effects. For instance, proponents of emotional intelligence argue that listening and responding to employee feelings (behaviors) builds trust and a sense of community (beliefs). Participative management is based on the view that greater employee involvement (behavior) increases their sense of ownership and commitment (values).

A Systems Approach to Motivation

The problem with emphasizing one or two motivational variables over others is that important information about why people do what they do can be lost or neglected. An excellent way to avoid this problem is by using *systems thinking*, which asks the practitioner to hold the whole in mind, consider the interactions of the component elements of the whole, and also to consider the relation of the whole to its larger environment.

There are closed and open systems. A closed system is isolated from its environment, while an open system receives inputs from its environment and acts on the environment through outputs. Human systems are open systems; they can't be understood completely through reductionistic, analytical thinking. Cognitive, affective and behavioral variables all contribute to motivation within the system; therefore it isn't necessary to figure out which variables are more important—or even what's a cause and what's an effect. The important thing is to consider them all, notice their dynamic interconnections, and use this information to foster positive change. The Motivational System Model does this.

The Motivational System Model, depicted in Figure 8.1, consists of four interrelated loops focusing on the personal, interpersonal, team, and organizational levels. The larger environmental context within which the four levels function. The larger context, which encompasses everything *outside* impacting the four levels, includes communities, economies, societies, and the world. Viewing organizations in this way is consistent with the OD Network's statement of values, which states: "We demonstrate our appreciation of systems by facilitating connectedness, a holistic approach and community" (see http://www.odnetwork.org/missionvalues.html). Also, most definitions of OD concern processes impacting individuals, work groups, and organizations (see, for example, Cummings & Worley, 2000; French & Bell, 1999). Burke (1997) described OD as *inter*, working between people and systems. Argyris (1997) stressed the importance of integrating the individual and the organization. Anderson and Ackerman-Anderson (2001) discussed the importance of focusing on the person and the organization in transformational change.

I refer to the personal loop as *personality*, and the interpersonal, team, and organization loops as three levels of organizational *culture*. The four levels become increasingly complex as we move from the personal to the organization. Overall organization culture is the most complex, because it includes all the individuals, interpersonal relationships, and teams within a whole organization.

Human systems have a natural tendency toward wholeness or integration (Morgan, 1986), but many factors, such as distorted facts and beliefs, negative feelings, and interpersonal conflict represent barriers to this. A good way to improve results, therefore, is to identify and minimize such barriers so the entire system can function more effectively. This requires an understanding of the personal, interpersonal, team, and organizational loops.

An individual moves around the personal loop a hundred or more times a day, usually without awareness of the movement or its underlying motivation. There's constant feedback among the variables as they endeavor to fulfill needs. Moreover, since people don't live in a vacuum—interpersonal relationships, teams, and organizations consist of individuals—complex interrelationships exist among the four loops. They're inextricably linked, representing four interdependent elements of a larger whole. Culture shapes personality; personality shapes culture.

The number of interactions and their complexity increases dramatically as we shift from the personal to the interpersonal and team levels, and becomes incalculable at the organizational level. To be effective, OD practitioners and other change agents must be able to shift their focus flexibly among these four levels of abstraction.

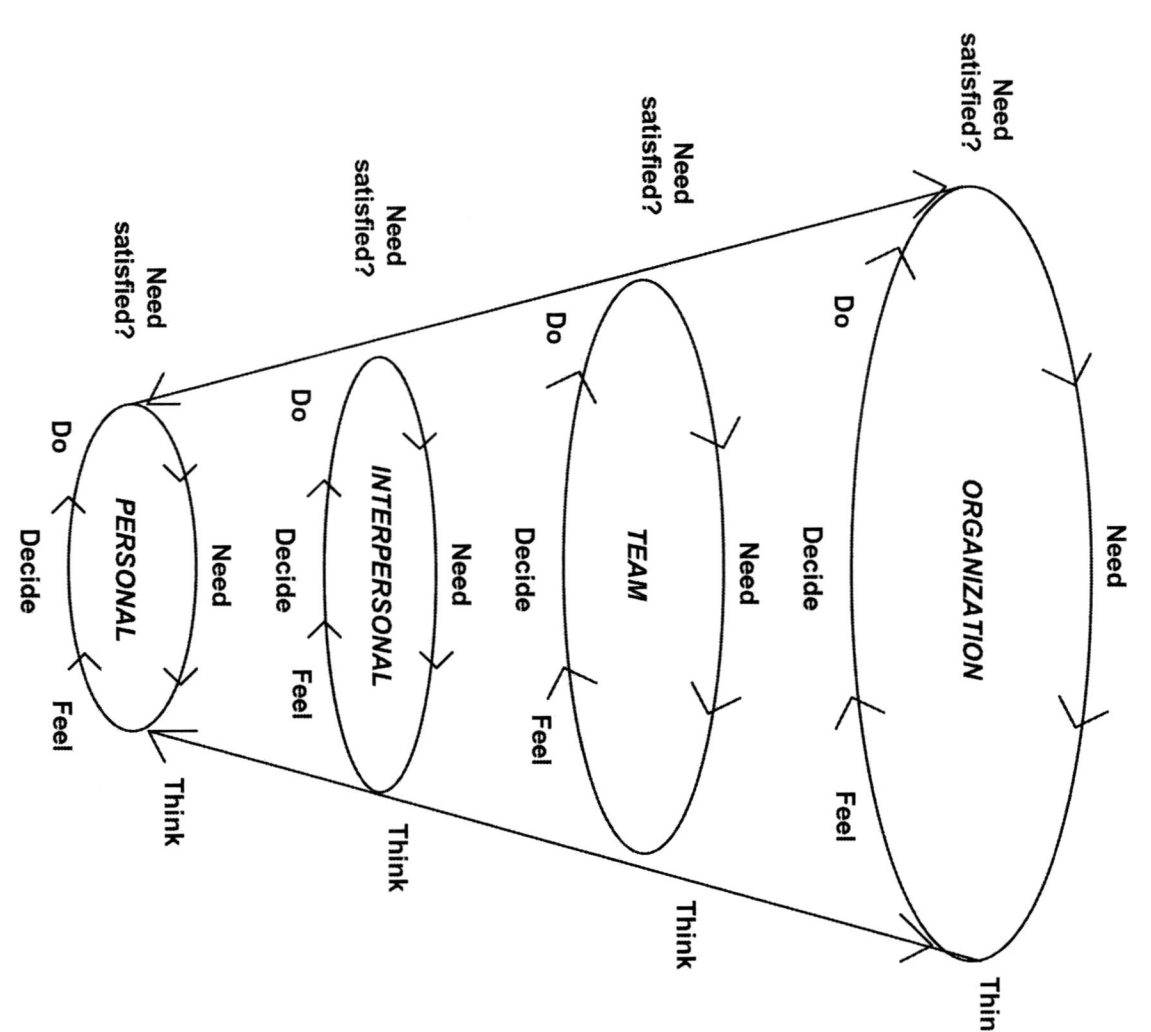

Figure 8.1
Motivational System Model

MOTIVATIONAL SYSTEM MAPPING™

Overview of Motivational System Mapping™

Motivational System Mapping (MSM) is a methodology for assessing the variables within the Motivational System Model (Hultman, 2002). It can be used to focus on any one of the four levels in the Model, or to look for relationships and disconnects among levels. It is intended to help people identify, organize, and use information relevant to their issues and concerns. This is done by asking questions to foster self-discovery, allowing people to retain responsibility for themselves, establish clarity about their vision, and take ownership of both the causes of and solutions to their problems.

Theoretical Foundation

The theoretical foundation for MSM has been laid in a variety of disciplines. In describing his theory of cognitive and behavioral change, Rokeach (1973) said, "A…method for inducing change is to expose a person to information about his own belief system, or to selected features of it, in order to make him consciously aware of certain contradictions that chronically exist within it below the level of awareness…information about contradictions within one's belief system that are perceived to be incompatible with self-conceptions should motivate cognitive and behavioral change that will remove or reduce incompetent or immoral self-conceptions" (pp. 233-234).

Consistent with this approach, Senge (1990) said, "A useful starting exercise for learning how to focus more clearly on desired results is to take any particular goal or aspect of your vision. First imagine that the goal is fully realized. Then ask yourself the question, 'If I actually had this, what would it get me?' What people often discover is that the answer to that question reveals 'deeper' desires lying behind the goal" (p. 164). The questions asked during MSM often tap into deeper meanings that increase self-understanding. For example, asking someone, "What's the most important thing in your life?", and following it up with, "Why is that important?" helps them get at something deeper within themselves. This allows the person to see what's driving what, and to focus more intently on deeper meanings and motives.

There's also some overlap between methods suggested by MSM and personal construct psychology, which focuses on identifying the constructs (beliefs and values) people use to understand themselves and their world. One approach is called *laddering*, which uses facilitative questions to help people process the meaning of their responses. A variation of this, called dialectical laddering, relies on a series of questions to help people identify and resolve value conflicts. Neimeyer (1993) described a dialectical ladder as, "…a ladder whose antithetical construct poles are reconciled in a higher order integration or synthesis. When such integration is successful, dialectical laddering provides not only an assessment of the structure of the client's current system, but also a series of guideposts pointing toward new potentials to be explored in therapy and in daily life" (p. 63).

A method like this can be useful when someone is experiencing a basic dilemma between two alternatives that both seem bad. In situations like these, it can be helpful to ask:

- *Can you find an alternative that would reconcile these two poles?*, and
- *How would that differ from the two polar extremes?*

Similarities also exist between MSM and cognitive therapy (see, for example, Beck, 1976, and Ellis, 1973). Cognitive therapists take the position that it's our interpretations of events that elicit emotional and behavioral responses. Emotional and behavioral problems are dealt with by challenging irrational beliefs, because they can distort our interpretations. A cognitive therapist plays an active role in challenging irrational beliefs and cognitive restructuring, skills requiring specialized training. In contrast, the MSM coach facilitates client self-assessment. While MSM undoubtedly has some therapeutic outcomes, its purpose is primarily developmental and educational.

MSM and Appreciative Inquiry

A brief comparison between MSM and Appreciative Inquiry (AI) might be useful, since the latter approach to OD is growing in popularity and influence. Instead of focusing on traditional problem-solving, AI seeks to find what's right in organizations. Watkins and Cooperrider (2000) described AI as, "An articulated theory that rationalizes and reinforces the habit of mind that moves through the world in a generative frame, seeking and finding images of the possible rather than scenes of disaster and despair" (p. 6). AI practitioners help organizations articulate key ingredients in past successes and then to use those as the basis for creating a positive future.

AI is a new movement in OD based on a philosophy of practicing the positive (see, for example, Watkins & Mohr, 2000; Cooperrider, *et al*, 2000), while MSM is a specific methodology for identifying and dealing with system issues. While AI leads organizations to a focus on the positive, MSM is a balance model that looks at both driving and restraining forces in the tradition of Kurt Lewin's force field analysis (Lewin, 1947). My experience indicates that personal, interpersonal, team, and organizational problems usually stem from underlying issues that can't be identified or resolved by focusing on the positive alone.

MSM is based on the belief that under favorable conditions—those encouraging self-acceptance and trust—people will naturally move toward growth; therefore, the process starts wherever the client is ready to work and builds from there. The goal is to construct a map of the relevant factors in a situation so patterns and relationships can be identified. These patterns and relationships then help to focus development.

Understanding can be distorted by guiding a client toward either the positive or the negative. MSM attempts to minimize distortion by having the client decide what direction to take. If the client wants to talk about the positive or the negative, MSM accommodates them either way. Thomas Head (2000) makes the point that AI eliminates resistance to change because of the positive focus. MSM lowers resistance because the client decides the direction.

This doesn't mean that MSM is value-free. No OD methodology is totally value-free, nor do I think this is desirable. Even if you only ask questions and refrain from offering recommendations, you steer the process, consciously or unconsciously, by the questions you choose. The important thing is to make your biases known. When I use MSM, my underlying biases are toward:

- Seeking balance within the Motivational System Model,
- Moving the Motivational System Model away from fragmentation and toward wholeness,
- Separating causes from symptoms of problems, and
- Focusing interventions on causes.

Also, while it's theoretically possible to use MSM by *only* asking questions, in actual practice I've never employed it this way. As I listen to a client, I gain insights into symptoms, causes, patterns and themes, consequences, and actions. I offer these insights when I think it's appropriate, although my bias is toward being patient, giving clients time to gain their own insights. I will also offer my own recommendations, based on my biases toward balance, wholeness, and remedies that deal with causes.

One final point is that a thin line exists between assessment and intervention (Argyris, 1970; Burke, 1982). MSM is essentially an assessment method, but people gain insights during the process that change them, and anything producing positive change represents an intervention. Change in one belief or value has an impact on other beliefs and values because they're structurally and functionally related. Regarding this, Harrison (1969, p. 66) said, "Concepts are too closely and complexly linked to change one or two relationships in isolation. One change leads to another, pretty soon a major reorganization is going on." While MSM produces insight, its overall goal is to encourage change that helps people and organizations actualize their potential more fully.

MSM with Individuals

A coach can use MSM to help a person gain in self-understanding, clarify personal/professional mission and vision, locate driving and constraining forces, and develop a strategy for serving mission and bringing vision into being. Specifically, individuals can:

1. Clarify their purpose (mission) and their dream for the future (vision)
2. Establish goals for serving purpose and actualizing vision
3. Identify their current needs/wants, facts, beliefs, feelings, values and behaviors
4. Identify patterns and themes among current needs/wants, facts, beliefs, feelings, values, and behaviors
5. Assess positive and negative consequences of current needs/wants, facts, beliefs, feelings, values and behaviors
6. Identify changes needed to build on the positive and deal with the negative
7. Develop a plan for personal development
8. Monitor results and make necessary adjustments

The key skills in MSM are knowing what questions to ask and classifying responses according to the variables in the Motivational System Model. For example, a question like, "What options do you see?" gets at beliefs and perceived facts. Following up with, "What do you want to do?" moves the discussion to values. Table 8.2, Navigating the Motivational System Model, provides examples of questions relating to the five variables: needs, thinking, feelings, deciding, and doing.

As the client responds to questions, the coach writes down all responses in the appropriate category on a MSM Worksheet (see below). The purpose of the Worksheet is to show how responses are categorized. In actual practice you will need much more space than is provided here. I suggest you place the headings on pieces of note paper or sheets of easel paper.

You can start your questioning anyplace, which is consistent with the system concept of *equifinality*. Morgan (1986) had this to say about equifinality: "Living systems have flexible patterns of organization that allow the achievement of specific results from different starting points with different resources in different ways" (p. 47). Most human problems can be looked at from more than one perspective and have more than one solution. Therefore, begin where the person is motivated to work and build from there.

As the process progresses the note paper begins to fill in, and the client sees patterns and relationships between bits of information—the "map" becomes easier to understand. Clients often have many "ah hahs" during this experience, discovering relationships between beliefs, feelings, values, and behaviors. They start synthesizing seemingly unrelated pieces of information, allowing them to work toward a deeper level of personal integration.

Change can be facilitated by asking questions about patterns/themes, positive and negative consequences, and possible actions. Some questions relating to these areas are:

Patterns/Themes:

What are the symptoms/causes?

What patterns or themes do you see emerging?

What connections do you see between these responses?

What relationships do you see between your values and feelings, feelings and beliefs, beliefs and values, values and behaviors?

Consequences:

What positive consequences do you see?

How can you capitalize on these consequences more fully?

What barriers exist?

How can you overcome or minimize these barriers?

Actions:

What actions can you take?

How would those actions allow you to fulfill your purposes/dreams?

What specifically are you prepared to do and by when?

What resources do you have?

What additional resources do you need, and how can you get them?

Table 8.2
Navigating the Motivational System Model

Get from ↓ \ To →	NEED	THINK	FEEL	DECIDE	DO
NEED	What are your needs? What needs are/aren't being satisfied? What are some of your other needs? How have your needs changed?	How could you satisfy your needs? Are there better ways to satisfy your needs? How will these changes in needs impact your thinking?	How would you feel if you couldn't satisfy that need?	How do you decide the best ways to satisfy your needs? How will these changes in needs impact your decisions?	Does that satisfy your needs? What do you get by doing that? How will these changes in needs impact your actions?
THINK	How does that thinking allow you to meet your needs? Does that thinking keep you from meeting your needs? Would changing those thoughts allow you to meet your needs? What impact does you thinking have on other's needs?	What do you think about yourself? What are your beliefs about that? What's another way of looking at this? What keeps you from changing your thinking? What do you think is going to happen? How do you know that's true? What would happen if you changed your thinking?	How do those thoughts make you feel? How would you feel If that happened? How would others feel if that happened?	What factors do you consider when making a decision? What other input will you need before making a decision? What thinking went into this decision? Who else should be involved in making this decision? How could you change that decision? How do you evaluate your decisions?	How could you put those thoughts into action? What keeps you from doing that? How could you improve your actions? What are the consequences of your behavior? What impact do your thoughts have on other's actions? How do you evaluate your actions?
FEEL	How strongly do You feel about satisfying that need?	How do your feelings affect your thoughts?	What are your feelings? What other feelings Do you have?	How do those feelings affect your decisions?	How do those feelings affect your actions?
DECIDE	How would that decision satisfy your needs? What impact does that decision have on other's needs? How do you decide what needs to focus on?	What thoughts led to that decision? What are the pros and cons? What would the costs/benefits be of that decision? What are the potential consequences of that decision? What are the trade-offs? Are they acceptable?	How do you feel about your decision? How would that decision make you feel? How will you feel if your decision doesn't work out? How do others feel about the decision? What concerns do you have about the decision?	What is your mission/vision? What is important to you? What criteria do you use in making decisions? What are your priorities? How could you improve your decisions?	How could you put those decisions into action? What do you want to do? What impact do your decisions have on what other's do? What are the most important things you can do?

Get From ↓ / To →	NEED	THINK	FEEL	DECIDE	DO
DO	How does this action allow you to satisfy your needs? What other actions could you take to satisfy your needs?	What's the thinking behind those actions? How well do the actions work? What else do you think you could do? How could you change your thinking?	How did you feel about doing that? How would you feel if those actions didn't work?	What impact do your actions have on your decisions? What impact do other people's actions have on your decisions?	What behaviors have you tried? What else could you do? What behaviors do you want to keep? What behaviors do you want to change? What new behaviors do you want to add?

How long MSM will take depends on the situation and the degree of insight people have about the issues. If someone is upset emotionally, they'll need to vent their feelings before getting into the questions. Answering the questions is a more analytical process, and emotions can cloud that process. Emotional issues must be dealt with before the person can focus on MSM. It will take people capable of more insight less time to go through the process than others. Also, it's easier for some people to be open and talk about feelings. I've worked with people who moved through the process in a few hours, while others took many meetings over a period of time. I prefer a marathon session away from the workplace, where the person can focus intently on their situation without interruptions. If you have an entire day set aside for this, you get a sense for whether or not it continues to be productive. If you reach a point of diminishing return, quit for the day and pick it up later.

At other times long sessions aren't feasible due to time constraints. At the end of a session, I leave all my notes with them to ponder until our next meeting. Often the person gains insights between sessions that help frame the next meeting. I tell them that the data are theirs, not mine, and that the information is confidential. When coaching concludes, I leave all my notes with the person. They sometimes refer back to their notes months or even years later, gauging progress and gaining additional insights. This builds self-confidence and helps them deal with new issues more effectively.

MSM with Teams and Organizations

MSM can also be used with teams and organizations. The questioning process allows a team to gain greater ownership of its issues and solutions. MSM has the added benefit of helping to foster greater trust and cohesiveness, because everyone is contributing in the process. It also can increase the integration or alignment among individual, team and organizational values, and enhance the team's confidence and skill in identifying and dealing with its issues. Specifically MSM can help a team or organization do the following:

1. Define or redefine its mission and vision
2. Establish goals for serving its mission and bringing its vision into being

3. Identify current needs/wants, facts, beliefs, feelings, values and behaviors

4. Identify patterns and themes among current needs/wants, facts, beliefs, feelings, values and behaviors

5. Assess positive and negative consequences of current needs/wants, facts, beliefs, feelings, values and behaviors

6. Identify changes needed to build on the positive and overcome the negative

7. Develop a plan for development and building alignment

8. Monitor results and make necessary adjustments

Motivational System Mapping™ Worksheet

NEEDS:	
THINKING: Facts	
Beliefs about self	
Beliefs about others	
Beliefs about the organization/external environment	
FEELINGS:	
DECIDING: Terminal values	
Instrumental values	
DOING (behaviors):	

Patterns/themes:

Consequences:

Actions:

The process with a team is much the same as with an individual. The major difference is that the focus of attention is on the team instead of a person. After clarifying expectations, I define the variables in the Motivational System Model (needs, thinking, feelings, deciding, and doing). I write the name of each variable at the top of a separate sheet of easel paper, and post them conspicuously around the room. Then I ask questions to generate information about the five motivational variables. Whenever someone makes a comment, I write it on the appropriate sheet of paper. As the sheets begin to fill up, members spot patterns and relationship among responses (sometimes I divide team members into subgroups and they generate this information on their own). Once their issues become clearer, members are then able to generate potential solutions. At the end of the session, I compile all the information and distribute it to team members.

It's common for information raised by different team members to be contradictory. In fact, one of the goals of MSM is to bring such differences out in the open. The discussions that occur during MSM are most constructive if people avoid disagreeing over the validity of each other's perceptions and simply see this as data. Many value conflicts between people or among members of a team occur because people become polarized in their positions. Such conflicts can often be resolved by helping them move from dualistic to dialectical thinking, seeking a synthesis of the different positions (finding common ground), or looking beneath the values causing conflict to locate deeper shared values.

When MSM is used with organizations, it is a powerful tool in helping systems transform themselves. I meet with the leadership team and take them through the process much as described in the section on working with teams. The difference is that they are focusing on the whole organization, not on the leadership team itself. There's often a lot at stake in these sessions, because everyone is affected by the outcome. Dialogue among leaders regarding the state of the organization and its future can be very intense and meaningful. The process serves as a reality-check on the viability of an organization's culture, helping leaders spot distorted or outmoded assumptions, values, and norms that are undermining morale, performance, and results.

Summary

It's crucial for OD practitioners and other change agents to have a thorough understanding of human motivation. Motivational theories have tended to focus on one or two variables, neglecting others that might help us understand more fully why people do what they do. Motivational System Mapping (MSM) uses a systems approach to assess five key variables in motivation: needs, thinking, feelings, deciding, and doing. The theoretical foundation for MSM was presented, and techniques for using it with individuals, teams, and organizations were described.

Appendix 1

FAIRNESS: THE KEY TO VALUES-DRIVEN CONFLICT RESOLUTION

George J. McCall

University of Missouri-St. Louis

PURPOSE: To make a case for the importance of perceived outcome and procedural fairness in organizational conflict resolution.

Throughout the pages of this book, values have been promoted as appropriate decision-making criteria in organizational development. Over the decades of OD (Blake & Mouton 1964; Walton 1969; Fischer, 1972) one important class of decisions has concerned the handling of organizational conflict, whether such conflicts are formal and public disputes (Brown 1983) or, especially in more recent years, hidden and private conflicts (Kolb & Bartunek, 1992; Morrill 1995). Conflict resolution through rational means was one of OD's earliest values (Schein & Bennis, 1965).

Needless to say, values (or more accurately, differences in values) are themselves often the issue in conflicts of all kinds (Kriesburg, 2003), including conflicts in work organizations (Liedtka, 1989). But more importantly for this book, many values—such as trust, consensus, efficiency—also serve as criteria for procedures for resolving conflicts, whether values-driven or not.

Among all such values, *fairness* (in the sense of showing no evidence of favoritism, self-interest, prejudice, or similar bias) surely ranks very high indeed (Fischer, 1997). In fact, unfair treatment is itself a leading provoker of employee complaints (Lipsky, Seeber, & Fincher, 2003). Many specific types of unfair treatment have been so important and recurrent that they have been targeted by numerous statutory provisions (e.g., acts regulating discrimination on the basis of age, race, or sex) and organizational policies (e.g., regulations against nepotism).

Fairness in resolving complaints is therefore a goal of all organizational conflict resolution efforts—fairness in both the outcomes reached and the procedures employed to reach them (Moore, 1986). Outcomes are regarded as fair (Rescher, 2002; Brams & Taylor, 1996) when they reflect what is properly due or merited—i.e., when outcomes are proportionate to rightful claims, at least in comparison with the outcomes and claims of the other participants in that conflict situation. In practice, of course, the moral principles that determine outcomes fairness, or distributive justice, too often involve substantial subjectivity, such that their very applicability itself requires prior negotiation among the parties.

But outcomes, even if not entirely satisfactory, are often accepted by participants if the procedures that generated those outcomes are themselves seen as fair—if, for example, conflict participants feel they had adequate opportunity to speak their piece, feel they were actually heard, feel they had some part in shaping the outcomes, and feel that the third party (if any) acted impartially (Lind & Tyler, 1988; Rohl & Machura, 1997). Because lack of satisfaction with outcomes can sometimes be overcome by satisfaction with the fairness of a dispute resolution process (Moore, 1986), procedural fairness has received much more attention than has outcomes fairness (Greenberg & Cropanzano, 2001). (Alternatively, perhaps, intervenors emphasize procedural satisfaction simply because they have more control over process than over what a party will or will not accept in the way of a substantive outcome.)

Traditionally in OD, conflict resolution interventions have taken the form of single-occasion or otherwise time-limited efforts (Brown, 1983; Fischer, 1972, 1997)—often stigmatized as a "band-aid" approach. Because conflicts are always instead a recurring organizational difficulty, organizational developers are today often asked to design a *system* of conflict resolution procedures suited to the character of a specific organization. Such systemic interventions, or "dispute resolution systems," were pioneered by Ury, Brett, and Goldberg (1988) and have become highly fashionable over the last decade or two (Costantino & Merchant, 1996; Lipsky, Seeber, & Fincher, 2003). (Critics, of course, contend that designing a DRS only puts in place a system for applying the same old band-aids.) But whether or how such a systemic intervention actually works, judgments of its procedural fairness clearly involve elements somewhat different from those of single-occasion interventions. A committee of the Association for Conflict Resolution has accordingly established the following eight essential elements for assuring procedural fairness in constructing dispute resolution systems (see Lipsky, Seeber, & Fincher, 2003):

1. Voluntariness

2. Protection of privacy and confidentiality

3. Impartiality of neutrals

4. Trained and qualified neutrals

5. Prohibition of retaliation

6. Protection of collective bargaining rights

7. Diversity and accessibility, and

8. Preclusion of statutory rights

Most importantly for my own work, and for the thrust of this book, certain social psychologists (both in sociology and in psychology) have found in procedural fairness an organizational variable that may bring out the best in members, so that members go beyond mere compliance with organizational rules to discretionary actions that further organizational effectiveness (Hegtvedt, Thompson, & Cook, 1993; Tyler & Blader, 2003). That is, procedural fairness has been found to contribute importantly to *identity factors* that count far more heavily than economic rewards in members so identifying with their work organization that they actively engage in promoting its welfare.

And of course, such an identity-based understanding of organizational behavior has long been an aim of our own role-identity theory (McCall & Simmons, 1978); role-identities go well beyond roles in illuminating what individuals actually do. For example, Weber's (1968) classical analysis of bureaucratic organization not only showed how this mode of organization simultaneously limits and induces organizational conflict, it did so by distinguishing between the office and the person—i.e., between role and player. Roles in such organizations are not only impartial but are also impersonal, explicitly neglecting the player. Yet it is never enough to know that Sally serves as an accounts clerk (a role); we must also know what *kind* of accounts clerk she thinks of herself as being, how she conceives of herself as an accounts clerk (a role-identity). Only then can an organization developer see and understand the hurts she may come to suffer and, from those hurts, the hidden conflicts (often values-driven) that sabotage and undermine the workings of the organization (Kolb & Bartunek, 1992; Morrill, 1995).

In sum, promoting a value such as fairness can bring out among the members of an organizational social system an identity-basis for their actions that enhances not only our understanding of their conflicts, but also the effectiveness of their organizational actions.

Steps for resolving conflict when you have an issue with someone, and when someone has an issue with you, are included in the Supplemental Guidelines section of Chapter 7.

BIBLIOGRAPHY

Anderson, D. & Ackerman Anderson, L. (2001). *Beyond change management: Advanced strategies for today's transformational leaders.* San Francisco, CA: Jossey-Bass/Pfeiffer.

Argyris, C. (1970). *Intervention theory and method.* Reading, MA: Addison-Wesley.

Argyris, C. (1997). *Integrating the individual and the organization.* New Brunswick, NJ: Transaction Publisher.

Badaracco, J. L., & Ellsworth, R. R. (1989). *Leadership and the quest for integrity.* Cambridge, MA: Harvard Business School Press.

Beck, A. (1976). *Cognitive therapy and emotional disorders.* Madison, CT: International Universities Press.

Beckhard, R., & Harris, R. T. (1987). *Organizational Transitions: Managing Complex Change (2nd Edition),* Addison Wesley: Reading, MA.

Bennis, W. G. (1969). *Organization development: Its nature, origins, and prospects.* Reading, MA: Addison-Wesley.

Bernstein, A. J., & Rozen, S. C. (1994). *Sacred bull.* New York: Wiley.

Blake, R. R. & Mouton, J. S. (1964). *The Managerial Grid.* Houston: Gulf.

Blanchard, K. H. & Peale, N. V. (1988). *The power of ethical management.* New York: Fawcett Columbine.

Block, P. (1996). *Stewardship: Choosing service over self-interest.* San Francisco, CA: Berrett-Koehler.

Bower, M. (1966). *The will to manage.* New York: McGraw-Hill.

Brams, S. J., & Taylor, A. D. (1996). *Fair Division: From Cake-Cutting to Dispute Resolution.* New York: Cambridge University Press.

Brehm, J. W. (1966). *The theory of psychological reactance.* New York: Academic Press.

Brown, L. D. (1983). *Managing Conflict at Organizational Interfaces.* Reading, MA: Addison-Wesley.

Buckingham, M., & Coffman, C. (1999). *First break all the rules: What the world's greatest managers do differently.* New York: Simon & Schuster.

Burke, W. W. (1982). *Organization development: Principles and practices.* Boston, MA: Little, Brown and Company.

Burke, W. W. (1997). The new agenda for organization development. *Organizational Dynamics,* Summer, 7-20.

Cable, D. M., & Judge, T. A. (1996). Person-organization fit, job choice decisions, and organizational entry. *Organizational Behavior and Human Decision Processes,* 67: 294-311.

Chao, G. T., O'Leary-Kelly, A. M., Wolf, S., Klein, H. J., & Gardner, P. D. (1994). Organizational socialization: Its contents and consequences. *Journal of Applied Psychology,* 79: 730-743.

Chatman, J. A. (1991). Matching people and organizations: Selection and socialization in public accounting firms. *Administrative Science Quarterly,* 36, 459-484.

Collins, J. C., & Porras, J. I. (1994). *Built to last: Successful habits of visionary companies.* New York: HarperBusiness.

Cooperrider, D., Sorensen, P., Whitney, D., & Yeager, T. (2000). *Appreciative inquiry.* Champaign, IL: Stipes Publishing.

Costantino, C. A. & Merchant, C. S. (1996). *Designing Conflict Management Systems: A Guide to Creating Productive and Healthy Organizations.* San Francisco: Jossey-Bass.

Covey, S. R. (1989). *The seven habits of highly effective people.* New York: Simon & Schuster.

Covey, S. R. (1990). *Principle-centered leadership.* New York: Simon & Schuster.

Cummings, T., and Worley, C. (2000). *Organizational development and change* (7th ed.). Cincinnati, OH: Southwestern College Publishing.

De Geus, A. (1997). *The living company: Habits for survival in a turbulent business environment.* Boston, MA: Harvard Business School Press.

Denison, D. (1984). Bringing corporate culture to the bottom-line. *Organizational Dynamics,* 13(2), 4-22.

Ellis, A. (1973). *Humanistic psychology: The Rational-emotive approach*, New York: Julian Press.

Executive Development Associates. (2004). *2004 trends in executive development survey*, San Francisco, CA.

Fischer, R. J. (1972). Third party consultation: A method for the study and resolution of conflict. *Journal of Conflict Resolution*, 16: 67-94.

Fischer, R. J. (1997). Third party consultation as the controlled stimulation of conflict. Pp. 192-207 in Carsten De Dreu and Evert Van De Vliert, editors, *Using Conflict in Organizations*. London: Sage.

Fitz-Enz, J. (1997). *The 8 practices of exceptional companies*. New York: AMACOM.

French, W. L. & Bell, C. H., Jr. *Organizational development* (6th ed.). Upper Saddle River, NJ: Prentice Hall.

Gellermann, W., Frankel, M. S., & Ladenson, R. F. (1990). *Values and ethics in organization and human systems development: Responding to dilemmas in professional life*. San Francisco: Jossey-Bass.

Gibb, J. R. (1964). Climate for trust formation. In Bradford, L.P., Gibb, J. R., & Benne, K. D. (Eds.), *T-group theory and laboratory method*. New York: John Wiley & Sons.

Golembiewski, R. T. (1972). *Renewing organizations: The laboratory approach to planned change*. Itasca, IL: F. E. Peacock Publishers, Inc.

Grant, L. (1998). Happy workers, High returns. *Fortune*, 139 (1), January.

Greenberg, J. & Cropanzano, R., Eds. (2001). *Advances in Organizational Justice*. Stanford, CA: Stanford University Press.

Greenleaf, R. K. (1991). *The servant as leader*. Indianapolis: The Robert K. Greenleaf Center.

Harris, S. G. & Mossholder, K. W. (1996). The affective implications of perceived congruence with culture dimensions during organizational transformation. *Journal of Management*, 22, 527-547.

Harrison, R. (1969). Defenses and the need to know. In W.B. Eddy, *et al.* (Eds.), *Behavioral science and the manager's role*, Washington, DC: NTL Learning Resources Corporation.

Harrison, R. (1970). Choosing the depth of organizational intervention. *Journal of Applied Behavioral Science*, 6, 181-202.

Head, T. C. (2000). Appreciative inquiry: Debunking the mythology behind resistance to change. *OD Practitioner*, 43(1).

Hegtvedt, K., Thompson, E. & Cook, K. S. (1993). Power and equity: What counts in attribution for exchange outcomes. *Social Psychology Quarterly*, 56: 100-119.

Herzberg, F. (1966). *Work and the nature of man*. Orlando, FL: Harcourt Brace.

Hultman, K. E. (1988). The psychology of performance management. *Training and Development Journal*, 42(7), 34-39.

Hultman, K. E. (1998). *Making change irresistible: Overcoming resistance to change in your organization*, Palo Also, CA: Davies-Black Publishers.

Hultman, K. (2002). *Balancing individual and organizational values: Walking the tightrope to success*, San Francisco: Jossey-Bass/Pfeiffer.

Kolb, D. M. & Barunek, J. M. Eds. (1992). *Hidden Conflicts in Organizations: Uncovering Behind-the-Scenes Disputes*. Newbury Park, CA: Sage.

Kotter, J. P. (1990). *A Force for Change: How Leadership Differs from Management*, New York: The Free Press.

Kotter, J. & Heskett, J. (1992). *Corporate culture and performance*. New York: The Free Press.

Kouzes, J. M & Posner, B. Z. (1995). *The leadership challenge: How to keep getting extraordinary things done in organizations*. San Francisco: Jossey-Bass Publishers.

Kriesburg, L. (2003). *Constructive Conflicts: From Escalation to Resolution* (2nd edition). Lanham, MD: Rowman & Littlefield.

Lawler, E. E. (1973). *Motivation in work organizations*. Monterey, CA: Brooks/Cole.

Lee, T. W., & Mowday, R. T. (1987). Voluntarily leaving an organization: An empirical investigation of Steers and Mowday's model of turnover. *Academy of Management Journal*, 30, 721-743.

Levering, R. and Moskowitz, M. (2000). 100 Best Companies to Work For. *Fortune*, 141 (1), January 10.

Levering, R. (2001). http://www.greatplacetowork.com/GPTWModel.htm.

Lewin, K. (1947). Group decision and social change. In T.N. Newcomb & E.L. Hartley (Eds.). *Readings in Social Psychology.* Troy, MO: Holt, Rinehart & Winston.

Liedtka, J. (1989). Managerial values and corporate decision-making: An empirical analysis of value congruence in two organizations. *Research in Corporate Social Performance and Policy,* 11: 59-91.

Lind, E. A. & Tyler, T. R. (1988). *The Social Psychology of Procedural Justice.* New York: Plenum.

Lipsky, D. B., Seeber, R. L. & Fincher, R. D. (2003). *Emerging Systems for Managing Workplace Conflict: Lessons from American Corporations for Managers and Dispute Resolution Professionals.* San Francisco: Jossey-Bass.

Madrick, J. (1995). *The end of affluence: The causes and consequences of America's economic dilemma.* New York: Random House.

Maslow, A. H. (1968). *Toward a psychology of being* (2nd Ed.). Princeton, NJ: D. Van Nostrand Company.

Massey, M. (1989). *What you are is where you were when…but not what you have to be.* Niles, IL: Nightingale-Conant.

McAniff, R. (1999). *The outrageous manager.* Polson, MT: McBliss & Associates.

McCall, G. J. & Simmons, J. L. (1978). *Identities and Interactions* (revised edition). New York: Free Press.

McClelland, D. C. (1975). *Power: The inner experience.* New York: Irvington.

McDougal, W. (1926). *An introduction to social psychology.* New York: John W. Luce.

Maurer, R. (1996). *Beyond the walls of resistance: Unconventional strategies that build support for change,* Bard Press: Austin, Texas.

Moomaugh, R. & Associates (1999). Reengineering: Why it so often fails. Valley Center, CA: Organizational Universe Systems.

Moore, C. W. (1986). *The Mediation Process: Practical Strategies for Resolving Conflict.* San Francisco: Jossey-Bass.

Morgan, G. (1986). *Images of organizations.* Thousand Oaks, CA: Sage.

Morrill, C. (1995). *The Executive Way: Conflict Management in Corporations*. Chicago: University of Chicago Press.

Moss-Kanter, E. (1985). *The change masters: Innovation and entrepreneurship in the American corporation*, Simon & Schuster: New York.

Neimeyer, R. A. (1993). Constructivist approaches to the measurement of meaning. In G.J. Neimeyer (Ed.) *Constructivist assessment: A casebook*. Thousand Oaks, CA: Sage.

O'Reilly III, C. A., Chatman, J. A., & Caldwell, D. F. (1991). People and organizational culture: A profile comparison approach to assessing person-organization fit. *Academy of Management Journal, 34*, 487-516.

Rescher, N. (2002). *Fairness: Theory and Practice of Distributive Justice*. New Brunswick, NJ: Transaction Books.

Rim, Y. (1970). Values and attitudes. *Personality, 1*, 243-250.

Rohl, K. F. & Machura, S. Eds. (1997) *Procedural Justice*. Aldershot: Ashgate.

Rokeach, M. (1968). *The three Christs of Ypsilanti*, New York: Knopf.

Rokeach, M. (1973). *The nature of human values*: New York: The Free Press.

Schein, E. H. (1992). *Organizational culture and leadership* (2nd ed.). San Francisco, CA: Jossey-Bass Publishers.

Schein, E. H. and Bennis, W. G. (1965). *Personal and organizational change through group methods: The laboratory approach*. New York: John Wiley & Sons.

Schiemann, W. (1992). Why change fails. *Across the Board*, April.

Senge, P. M. (1990). *The fifth discipline: The art & practice of the learning organization*. New York: Doubleday.

Senge, P. M. (1994). *The fifth discipline fieldbook*. New York: Doubleday.

Senge, P. M., et al (1999). *The dance of change: The challenge of sustaining momentum in learning organizations*, Doubleday: New York.

Shaw, R. B. (1995). *Trust in the balance: Building successful organizations on results, integrity, and concern.* San Francisco: Jossey-Bass.

Tannenbaum, R. and Davis, S. A. (1969). Values, man and organizations. In W. B. Eddy, *et al.* (Eds.), *Behavioral Science and the Manager's Role,* Washington, D.C.: NTL Learning Resources Corporation, 3-24.

Tyler, T. R. & Blader, S. (2000). *Cooperation in Groups: Procedural Justice, Social Identity, and Behavioral Engagement.* Philadelphia: Taylor & Francis.

Ury, W. L., Brett, J. M. & Goldberg, S. (1988). *Getting Disputes Resolved: Designing Systems to Cut the Costs of Conflict.* San Francisco: Jossey-Bass.

Vaill, P. (1996). *Learning as a way of being.* San Francisco: Jossey-Bass. Vroom, V. (1964). *Work and Motivation.* New York: Wiley.

Walton, R. E. (1969) *Interpersonal Peacemaking: Confrontations and Third-Party Consultation.* Reading, MA: Addison-Wesley.

Watkins, J. M. & Cooperrider, D. Appreciative inquiry: A transformative paradigm. *OD Practitioner, 32*(1), 6-12.

Watkins, J. M. and Mohr, B. J. (2000). *Appreciative inquiry: Change at the speed of imagination.* San Francisco, CA: Jossey-Bass/Pfeiffer.

Weber, M. (1968 [1922]). *Economy and Society* (Roth, G. and Wittich, C, Eds). Berkeley: University of California Press.

978-0-595-39394-7
0-595-39394-2

CPSIA information can be obtained at www.ICGtesting.com
Printed in the USA
LVOW051910290911

248476LV00002B/2/A